Buddy Rich's Rudiments Around the Kit

BY TED MACKENZIE

AF120241

To access companion content online, visit:
www.halleonard.com/mylibrary

Enter Code
3759-7075-6540-6338

Cover and page 4 photos: Getty Images
Project editor: David Bradley
Interior design and layout: Len Vogler

ISBN 978-0-8256-3727-8

This book Copyright © 2009 by Amsco Publications
International Copyright Secured All Rights Reserved

No part of this publication may be reproduced in any form or by
any means without the prior written permission of the Publisher.

Visit Hal Leonard Online at
www.halleonard.com

World headquarters, contact:
Hal Leonard
7777 West Bluemound Road
Milwaukee, WI 53213
Email: info@halleonard.com

In Europe, contact:
Hal Leonard Europe Limited
1 Red Place
London, W1K 6PL
Email: info@halleonardeurope.com

In Australia, contact:
Hal Leonard Australia Pty. Ltd.
4 Lentara Court
Cheltenham, Victoria, 3192 Australia
Email: info@halleonard.com.au

CONTENTS

Foreword 4

Introduction 5

Seated Behind the Kit 6

Key 8

Lesson 1
Balance Around the Kit 9

Lesson 2
Unison 11

Lessons 3–6
Single Strokes 12

Lessons 7–8
Accents 16

Lessons 9–18
The Three-Stroke Ruff 17

Lessons 19–27
The Four-Stroke Ruff 26

Lessons 28–35
The Five-Stroke Ruff 35

Lessons 36–44
The Five-Stroke Roll 43

Lessons 45–50
The Seven-Stroke Ruff 49

Lessons 51–58
The Seven-Stroke Roll 55

Lessons 59–64
The Nine-Stroke Ruff 60

Lessons 65–73
The Nine-Stroke Roll 66

Lessons 74–76
The Double-Stroke Roll 72

Lesson 77
The Press Roll 76

Lessons 78–83
The Single Paradiddle 76

Lessons 84–89
The Double Paradiddle 81

Lessons 90–95
The Triple Paradiddle 86

Lessons 96–105
The Flam 91

Lessons 106–112
The Drag 101

Lessons 113–120
The Ruff Paradiddle 106

Lessons 121–128
The Single Ratamacue 112

Lessons 129–133
The Double Ratamacue 117

Lessons 134–138
The Triple Ratamacue 119

Lessons 139–143
The Compound Stroke 122

Lesson 144
Exercises in Triplets 125

FOREWORD

Buddy Rich, the "world's greatest drummer," will always be the benchmark of drumming. We must consider his God-given talent a supreme gift that all drummers must listen to, observe, recognize, admire, study, attempt to imitate, to the best of our ability.

Buddy Rich's Modern Interpretation of Snare Drum Rudiments, written in collaboration with Henry Adler, was first published in 1942. It remains the most comprehensive snare drum book ever written. A best seller since 1942, it has enlightened generations of drummers and will continue to do so for generations of drummers to come. *Buddy Rich's Rudiments Around the Kit* simply applies his rudiments from the original snare drum book to the drum kit. This is not an attempt to break down Buddy's stylistic approach. It will, however, equip drummers with a complete vocabulary to use at will, as their individual expression on the kit demands.

I strongly advise the student to first develop the skills taught in *Buddy Rich's Modern Interpretation of Snare Drum Rudiments* (by Buddy Rich, written in collaboration with Henry Adler, revised by Ted MacKenzie; Amsco Publications, New York, 2006) before attempting *Buddy Rich's Rudiments Around the Kit*. It is the bible of snare drumming.

It can be proven that everything a drummer plays, regardless of the drummer's ability, is a rudiment. Compared to melodic instruments, rudiments are the drummer's scales and chords. Buddy Rich's rudiments, designed to work in a very fluid manner around the drum set, work extremely well individually or combined. There is no favoring of the downbeat. Once these rudiments have been developed and applied to the kit, there will be no hesitation in leading with the left or right hand in the downbeat.

Rudimental marching drumming was the snare drum system that evolved into the drum set. Most all drummers in the swing era learned from rudimental snare drummers. The rudiments Buddy Rich used in his snare drum book are here for application to the drum set. *Buddy Rich's Rudiments Around the Kit* begins the drummer's process of developing rudiments on the drum set. Once you have applied these rudiments to the drum set, your new vocabulary will then enable you to play musically what you hear. Each rudiment could have been expanded on, but that is your expression to find!

TED MACKENZIE

Buddy Rich

INTRODUCTION

The basic drum set is a relatively new instrument. It incorporates five separate instruments: snare drum, hi-hat, bass drum, tom-toms and cymbals. The snare drum was the first component. It is the center of the kit, and had its start somewhere in the 15th or 16th century. Called a *tabor*, it was a two-headed drum with a single strand stretched across the bottom head, distinguishing it from an ordinary hand drum. For centuries, the snare drum was mostly used to organize military operations.

The beginning of the drum set began with the snare drum stand. Invented in the late 1800s, it changed the stance of the drummer. For the first time, the drummer was able to sit down to perform.

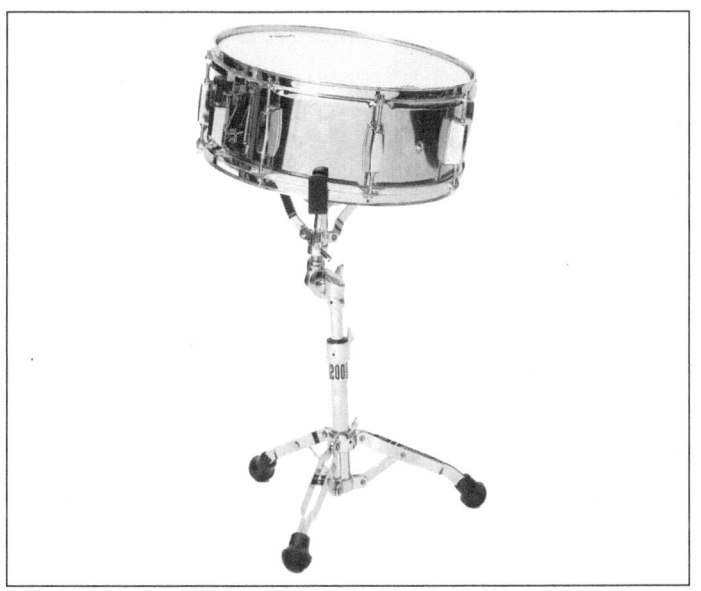

The bass drum pedal came next in 1906. Invented by William F. Ludwig, it was a major development. The bass drum pedal equipped the snare drummer with the ability to drive the band by subdividing the snare drum rudiments with the downbeat in the foot.

The hi-hat stand was the next development, allowing the drummer to subdivide the bass drum downbeat by rocking the heel and toe in time with the bass drum beat. The toe delivers a closed hi-hat downbeat, with the heel supplying a "silent" downbeat (opening the hi-hat), in time with the bass drum.

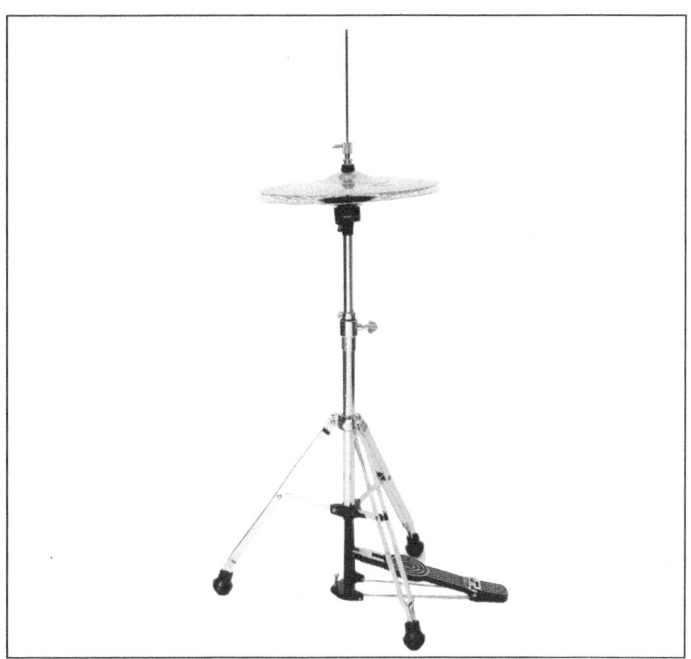

Tom-toms gradually gathered around the snare and bass drum, giving color to the new configuration. Cymbals were also evolving and "planted" around the drum kit in various configurations, giving the drum set sizzling accents and crashes. The development of the ride cymbal during the thirties and forties was the crowning glory of the modern drum set.

SEATED BEHIND THE KIT

Setup

It is of utmost importance to be comfortable and relaxed while seated at the drum set. Sitting at the correct height is the first consideration. Some drummers, who are sitting low, might tell you about "getting a nosebleed" if you sit too high. Actually, sitting too high could cause the edge of the seat to cut off the blood circulation to the legs. Sitting at the right height enables the drummer to relax the feet on the bass drum and hi-hat pedals without the knees getting in the way of the arms. The hip should be in line with the knee. The ankle and toe should be in line with the hip. The heel is placed directly under the knee. The foot and toe, resting on the bass drum pedal, are aligned to the bass drum.

The bass drum pedal should be firmly attached to the bass drum hoop. The spring on the bass drum pedal should be fairly loose, so you aren't making excess effort in striking the bass drum. When practicing, always allow the beater to release after striking the bass drum head. Using the "heel down" method is the best way to begin these studies. Strike and release the bass drum head with light, fast strokes.

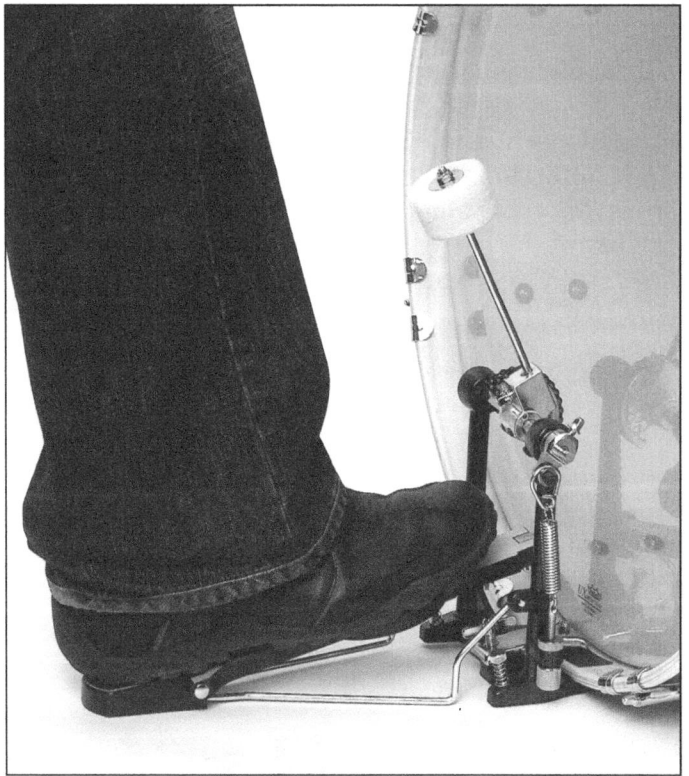

With the snare drum between the legs, place the sticks on the center of the drum. While leaving the tips of the drumsticks on the snare drum head, lower both sticks to the snare drum rim (rim shot position). Now, raise the sticks to just a millimeter off the snare drum rim. This position allows maximum stick rebound while giving access to the rim for rim shots. Be sure your hands and drumsticks are not touching any clothing, resting on, or rubbing the legs. In the same manner, adjust the toms and cymbals for minimal reach and maximum rebound.

The hi-hat is on the other side of the snare drum, with the heel resting on the heel plate of the hi-hat pedal. The heel must be directly underneath the knee. This allows the weight of the leg to work the hi-hat. With the leg completely relaxed, aggressively lift the heel, shifting the weight of the leg suddenly to the toe. This will give the "chick," or backbeat of the hi-hat that subdivides every other beat of the bass drum rhythm. The height of the hi-hat will depend on the height of the snare drum. The hi-hat is typically higher than the snare drum. The arm should be relaxed, with the tip of the drumstick on the bow of the top cymbal, in the maximum rebound position.

The ride cymbal should be in line with the arm, so there is no reaching. If the wrist is elevated too high, the lack of circulation will cause discomfort, slowing you down. The stick must be almost parallel to the cymbal for maximum rebound. Crash cymbals must be within easy reach.

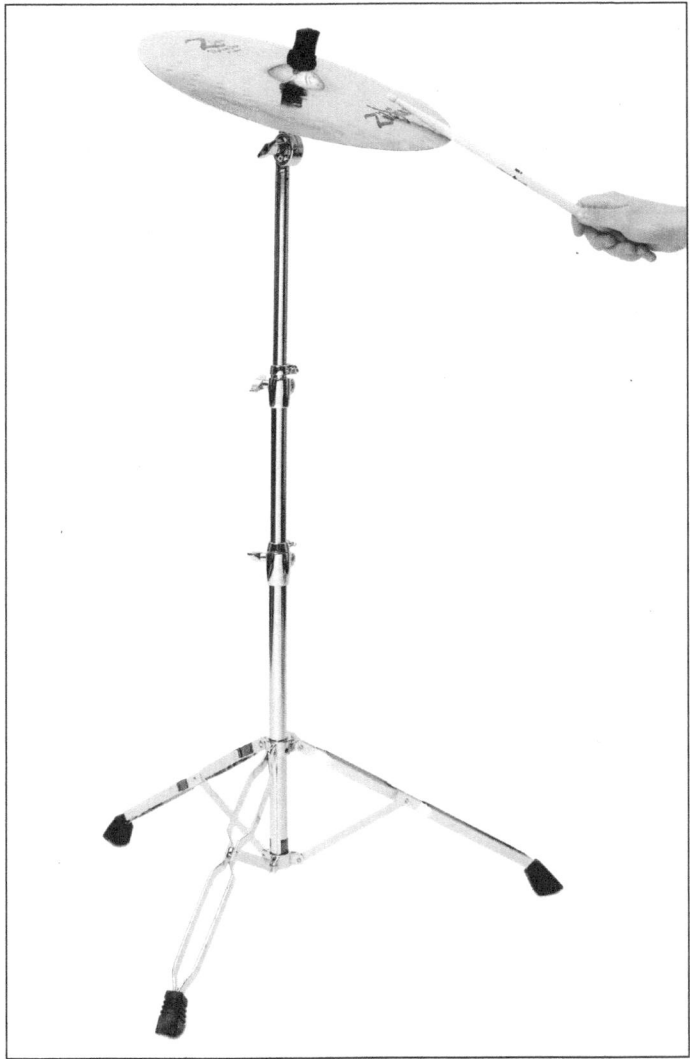

The Hands

Begin with a slow metronomic tempo to sustain the rhythmic model with a relaxed, balanced feel. When ready, reset the metronome to a slightly faster tempo. Resist sliding up to a faster tempo. Take care in not accenting the snare drum when tapping the bass drum. When accents are added, make them just a little louder than your "normal" strokes. When ready, work on rim shots in place of accents.

Wire brushes can be used. They offer low volume that will organize the hands while building stamina and strength. Because of the soft volume produced with wire brushes, essential subdivisions performed with the feet are now out in the open. *The Ultimate Drummer's Workout* (written by Ted Mackenzie; Amsco Publications, New York, 2006) was developed to increase the student's rudimental efficiency, and can be used in conjunction with *Buddy Rich's Modern Interpretation of Snare Drum Rudiments* and *Buddy Rich's Rudiments Around the Kit*.

The Arms

The arms deliver the sticks to the toms and cymbals. Be sure to be relaxed, using only the muscles needed to deliver the tips of the sticks to the "sweet spots" of the drums and cymbals.

The Feet

The feet are the foundation upon which the hands are built. Every rudiment presented here can be combined and "in time" as long as the feet are played as written. A light tap with the bass drum, and the hi-hat foot rocking heel and toe with each bass drum tap, subdividing the bass drum beat, is used throughout this study. Use extra height with the hi-hat heel, aggressively working with its timing in the bass drum downbeat. A fast "chick" with the hats makes a more aggressive player. Dropping the heel with exact timing on the bass drum downbeat secures the driving rhythm of the bass drum.

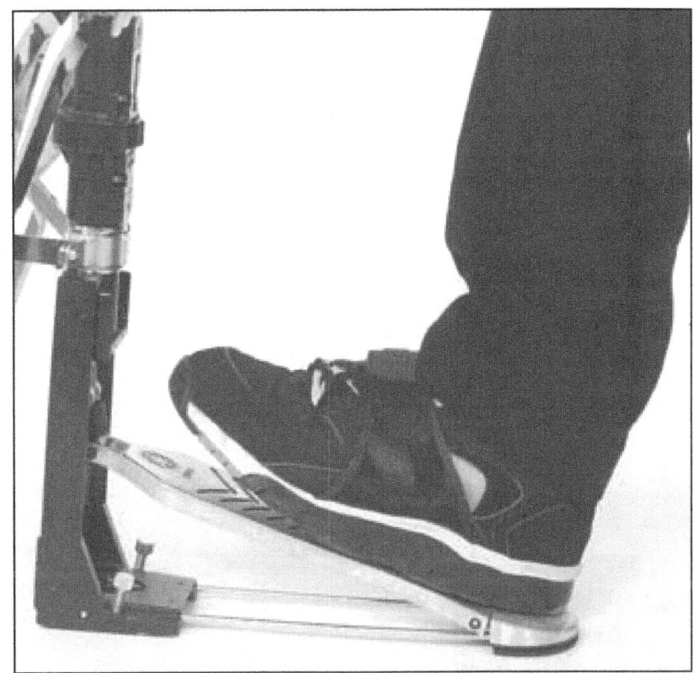

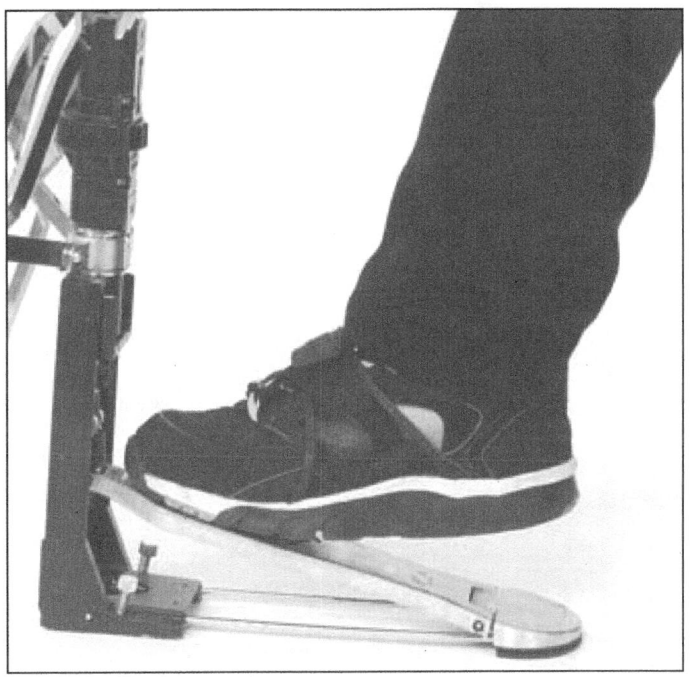

KEY

(R) Crash cymbal
(L) Crash cymbal
Tom-tom
Snare drum
Floor tom
Bass drum
Hi-hat
(R) Crash cymbal
(L) Crash cymbal
Tom-tom
Snare drum
Floor tom
Bass drum
Hi-hat

crash cymbal
ride cymbal
tom-tom
hi-hat
floor tom
snare drum
bass drum

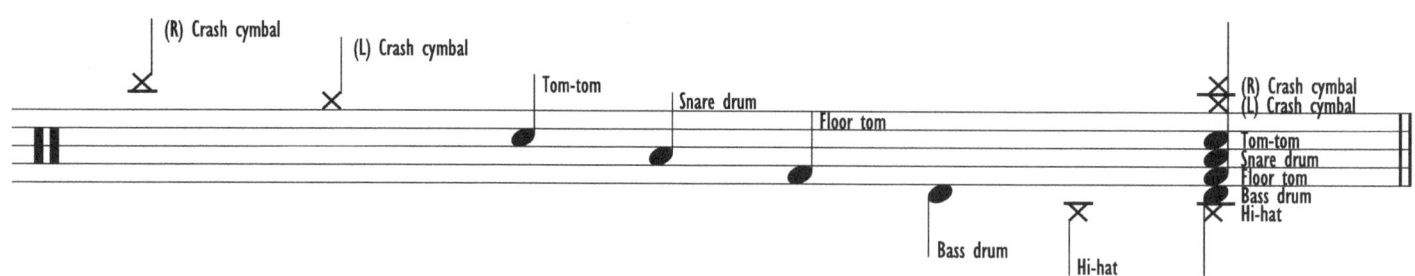

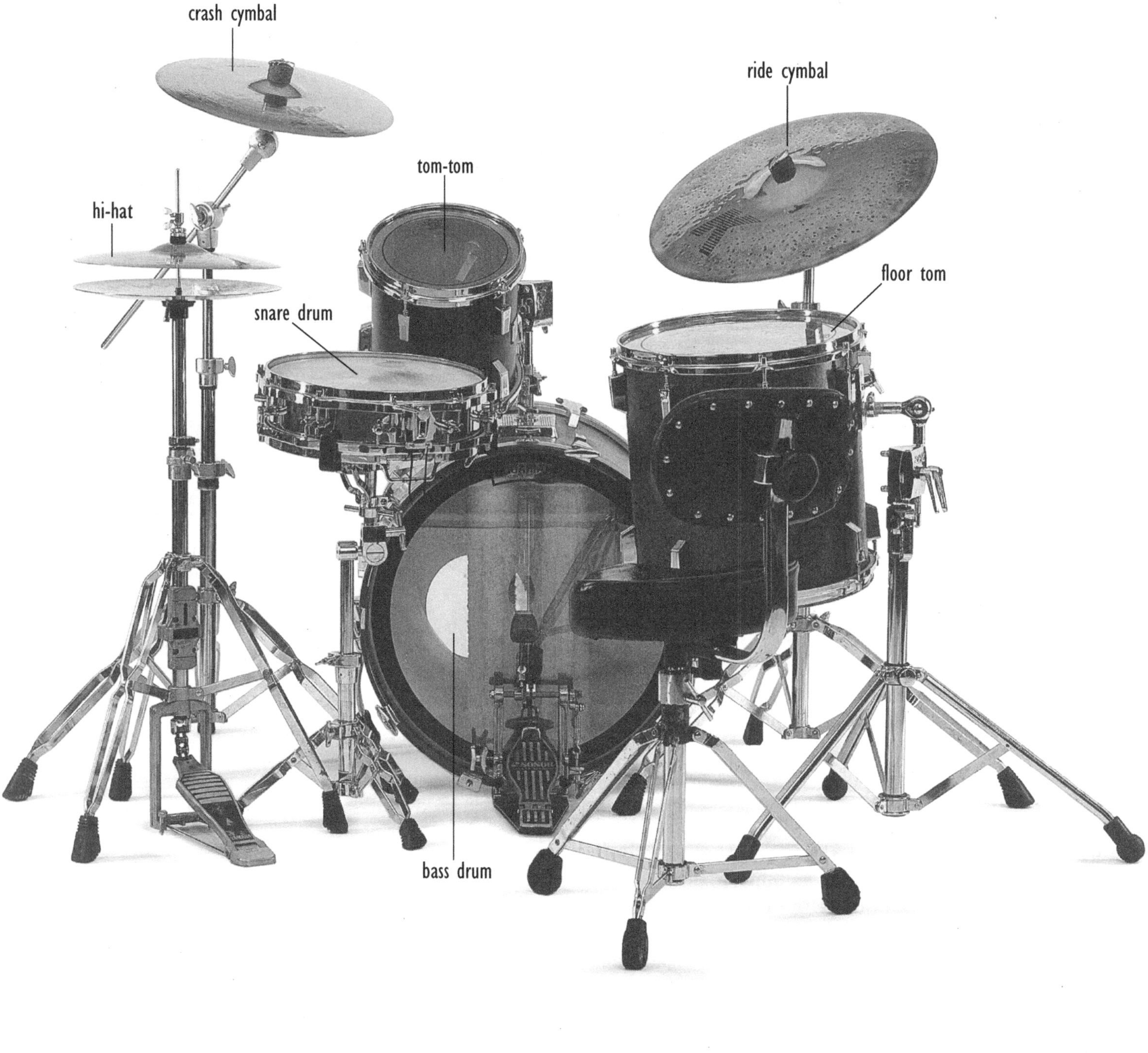

LESSON 1
Balance Around the Kit

Begin with slow, non-accented bounced strokes that are equal in volume and height. Tempo will be determined by the ability to accurately execute consistent snare drum figures while subdividing with the bass drum and hi-hat. Set metronome beats per minute (BPM) accordingly.

A simple way to remember the evenness of triplets is to say the word "e-ven-ly" aloud as you practice these figures with the metronome. Keep track of your progress and re-evaluate every few days.

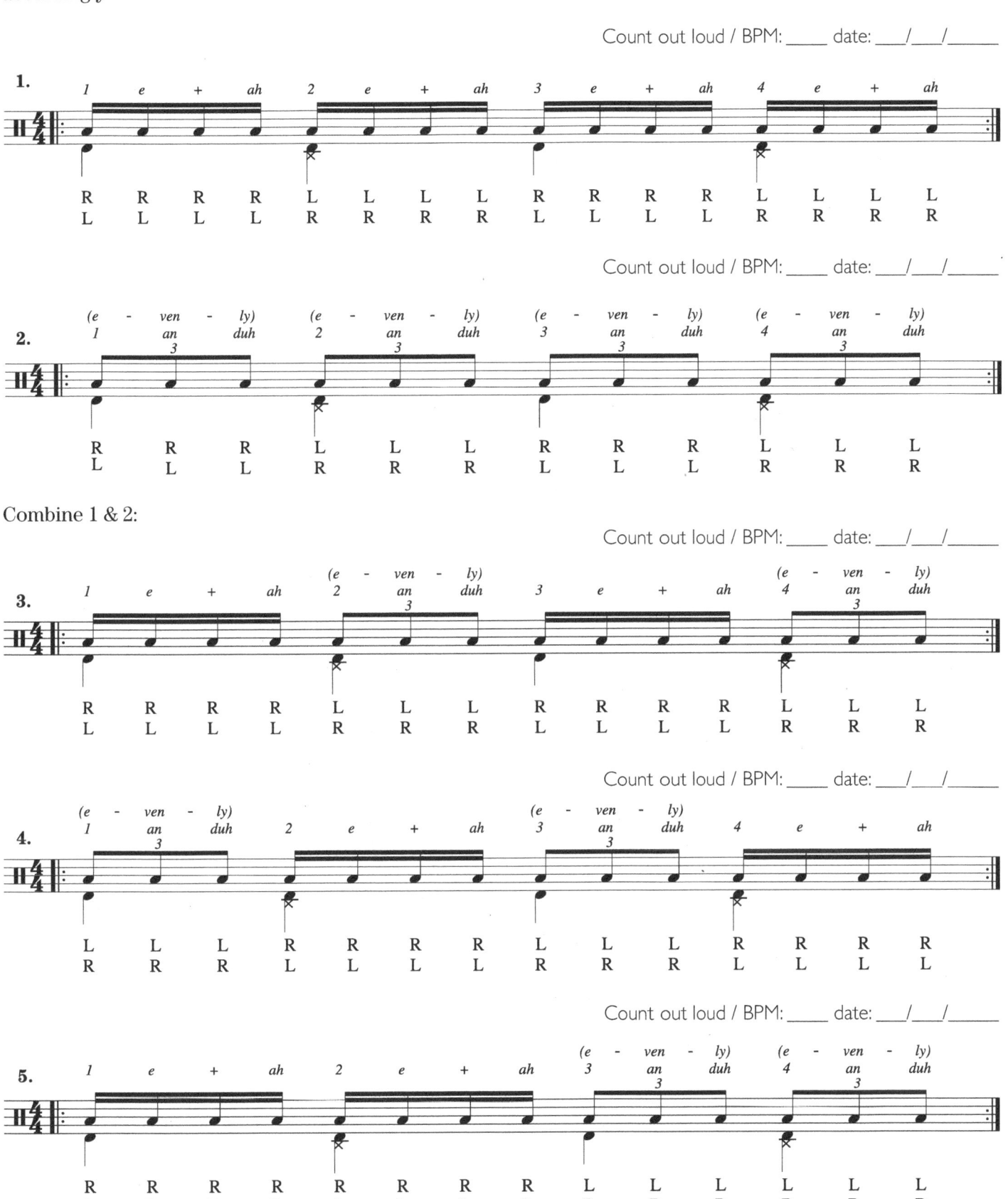

Combine 1 & 2:

Combine 7 & 8:

10

LESSON 2
Unison

Strike two drums at the same time. Be careful not to flam.

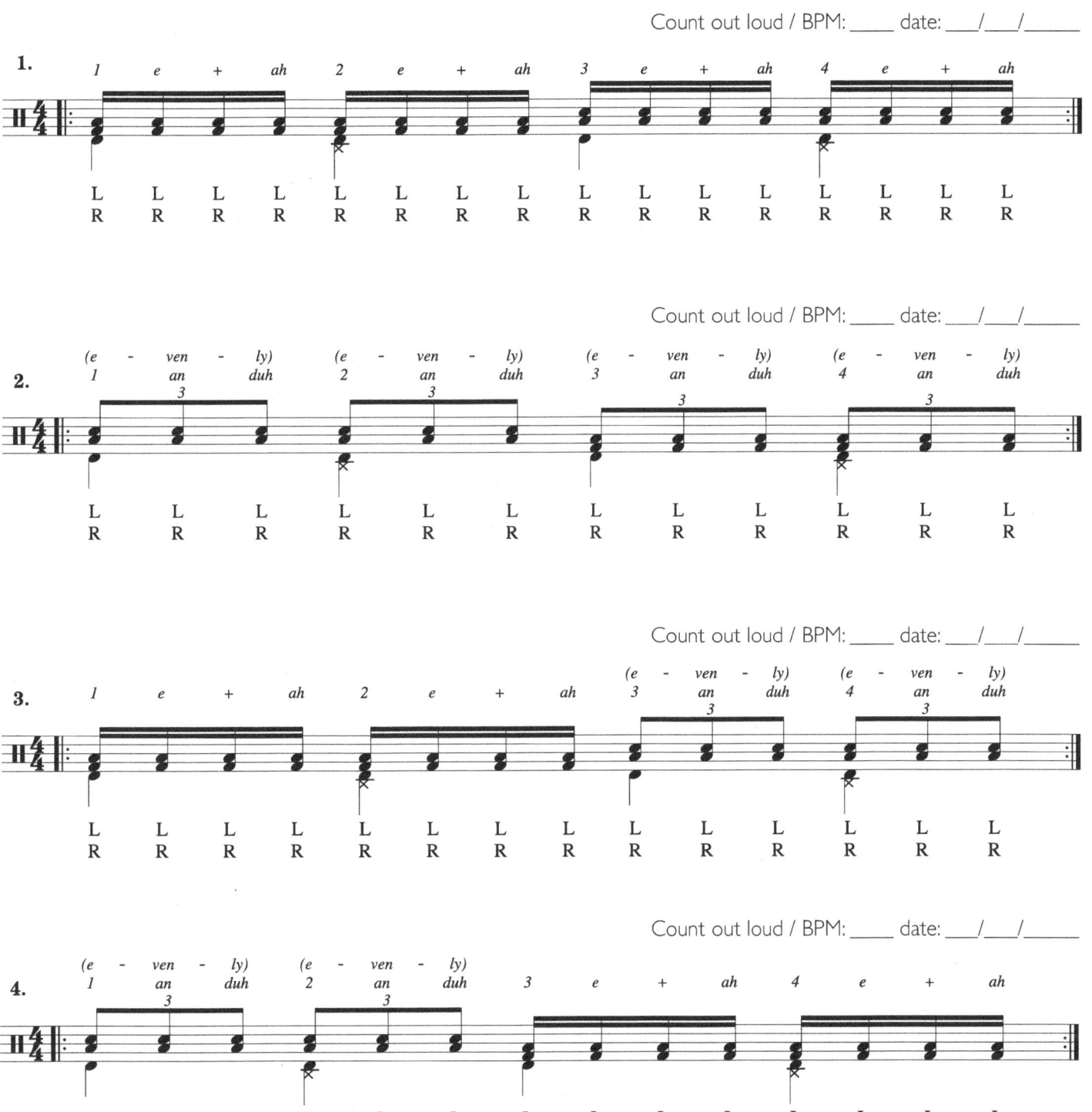

LESSON 3
Alternating Single Strokes

This most important rudiment must be executed with even, relaxed, full unaccented bounced strokes. Remember to move the wrists to each drum, with the whole arm as an extension of the drumstick.

LESSON 4
Alternating Single-Stroke Roll Around the Kit

All strokes must be played evenly with the same amount of volume, relaxed, with no change in rhythm before increasing tempo.

LESSON 5
Separating the Alternating Single-Stroke Roll

When separating hands, be sure the dynamics are equal without deviating from the rhythm.

Reverse:

LESSON 6
Alternating Single-Stroke Roll

With bass drum and snare drum; rocking heel & toe on the hi-hat, closing on *2* & *4*. On the count of *1*, drop in your heel on the hi-hat heel plate, followed by the toe closing the hats on the *2* count.

16ths with bass drum on downbeats:

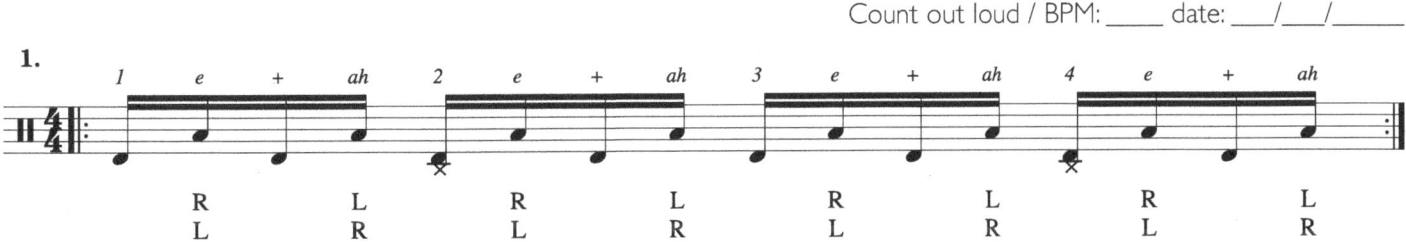

16ths with snare drum on downbeats:

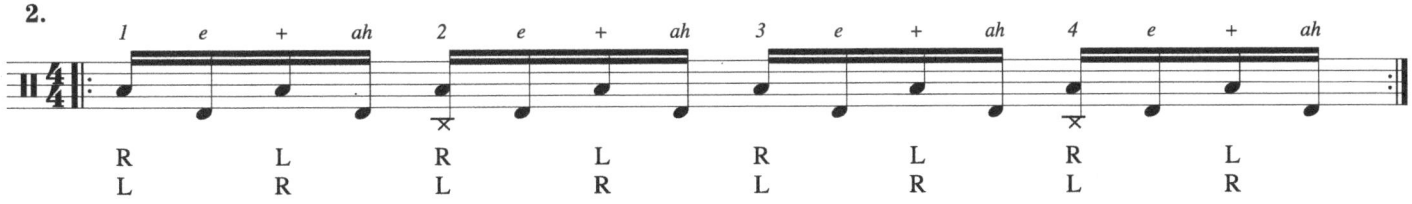

8th-note triplets:

Combine 1 & 3:

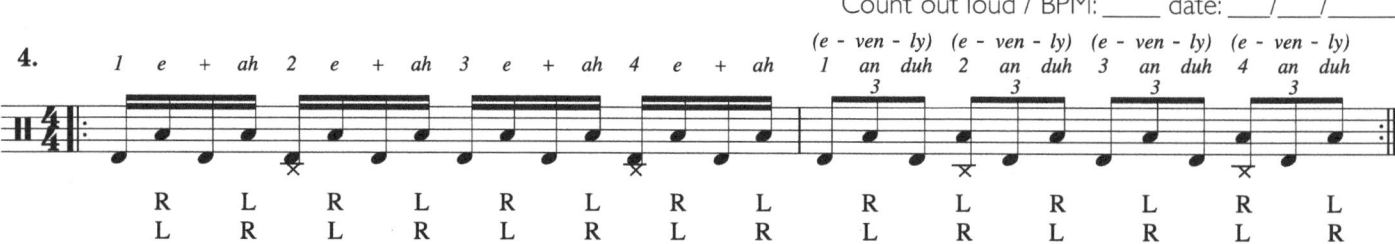

Combine 2 & 3:

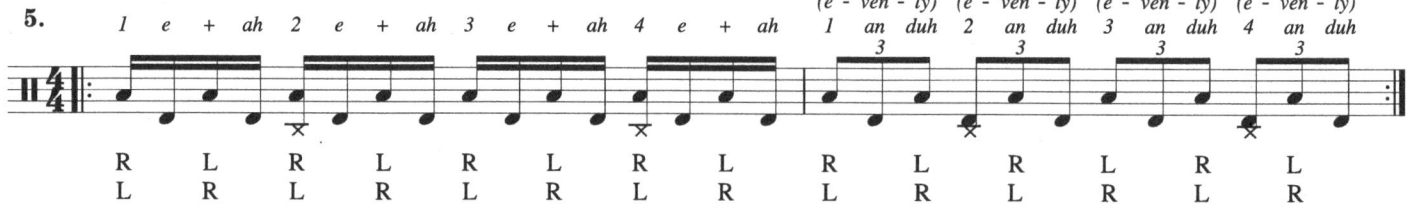

LESSON 7
Accents

All unaccented notes are relaxed full strokes. Accented strokes are all the same volume. Begin with a slower BPM than you think you need. Accuracy is more important than speed.

LESSON 8
Accents with Bass Drum

Do not bury the bass drum beater on the head. Feather the bass drum and snap the accented strokes.

LESSON 9
The Three-Stroke Ruff

Bass drum is on first and last beat of the phrase. Subdivide the bass drum with the hi-hat. After developing the accents, deliver the accented strokes to toms and cymbals.

Rhythmic model:

Three-stroke ruff with accent on last beat of phrase:

Three-stroke ruff with accent on first beat of phrase:

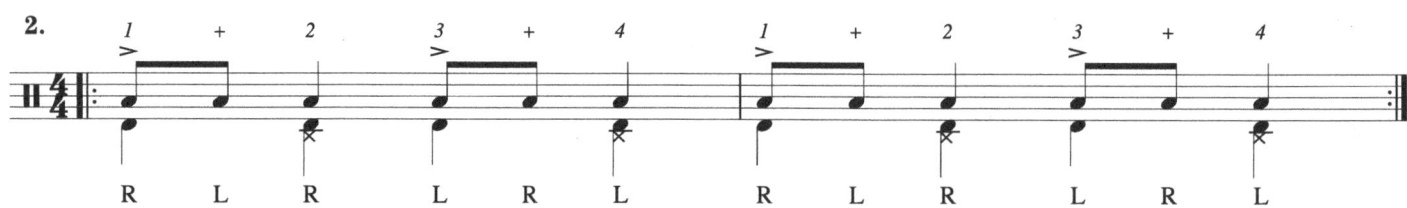

Combination of the accented three-stroke ruff:

LESSON 10
The Three-Stroke Ruff

Substitute toms in place of accents.

With toms at end of phrase:

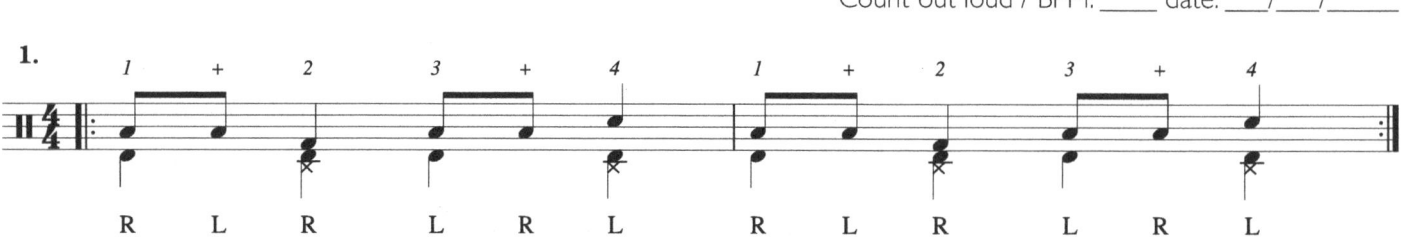

With toms at beginning of phrase:

Combine 1 & 2:

Reverse, with snare drum receiving the accents:

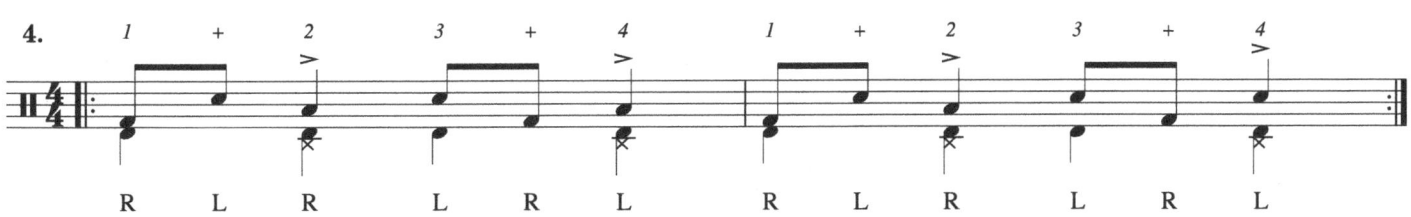

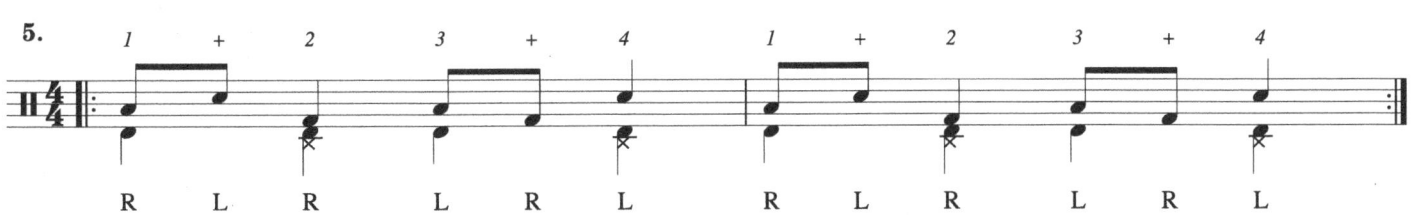

Combine 4 & 5:

LESSON 11
The Three-Stroke Ruff

Separate hands, with one hand per drum. Listen carefully to the change of expression.

Floor tom and snare drum:

Snare drum and tom-tom:

Floor tom and tom-tom:

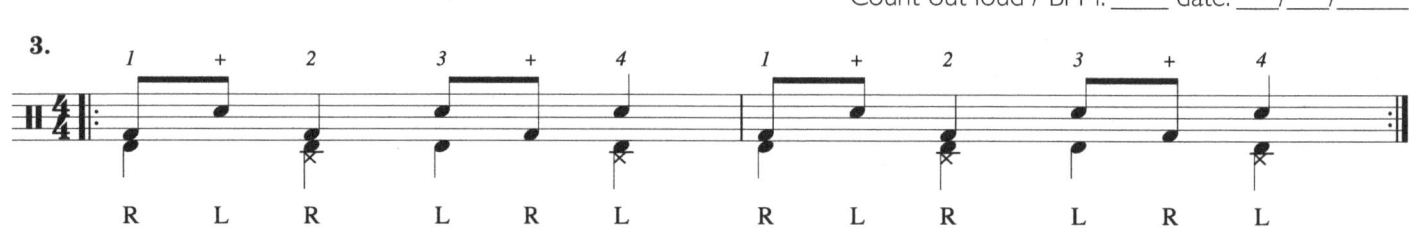

Combinations:

20

LESSON 12
The Three-Stroke Ruff

With crash cymbals on first beat and last beat of the phrase. Feather the bass drum; accent bass drum on cymbal crashes.

With crash cymbals and bass drum on first beat of phrase:

Count out loud / BPM: _____ date: ___/___/_____

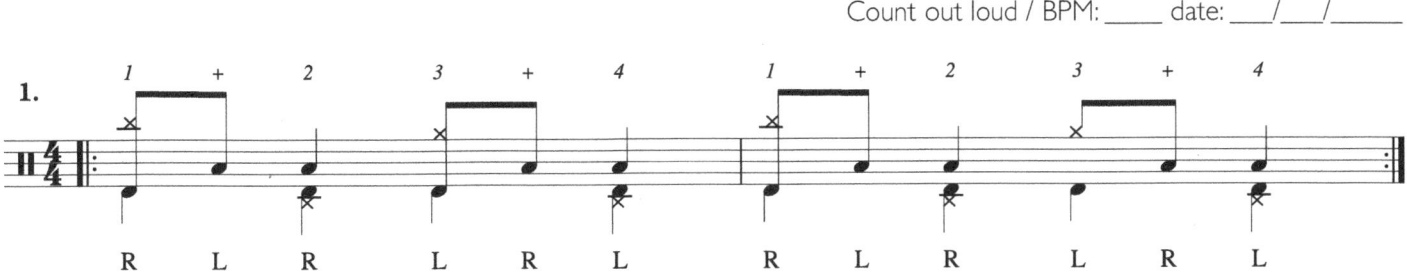

With crash cymbals and bass drum on last beat of phrase:

Count out loud / BPM: _____ date: ___/___/_____

Combine both exercises:

Count out loud / BPM: _____ date: ___/___/_____

LESSON 13
The Three-Stroke Ruff

With bass drum on the *and* (+) of *2* and the *and* of *4*, work out your rhythmic accuracy while carefully developing accents.

Rhythmic model:

Accent the third beat:

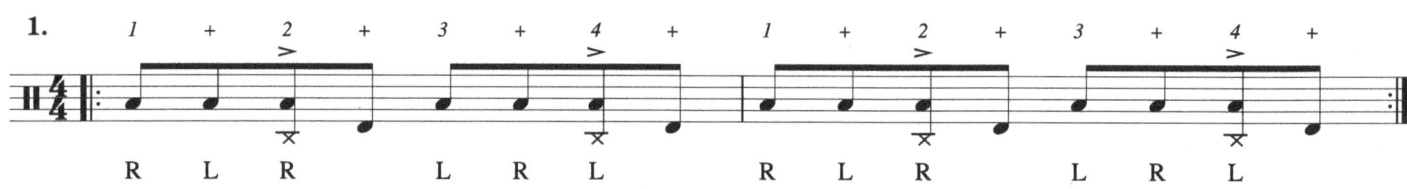

Accent the first beat:

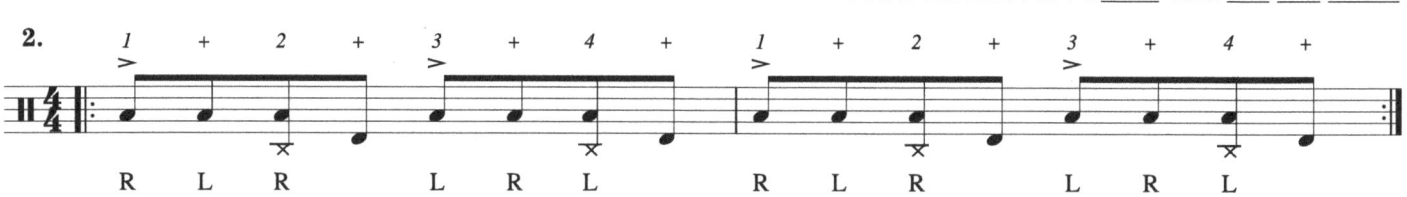

Combination of accents:

22

LESSON 14
The Three-Stroke Ruff

Substitute accents with toms.

Floor tom and tom-tom share first stroke:

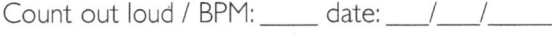
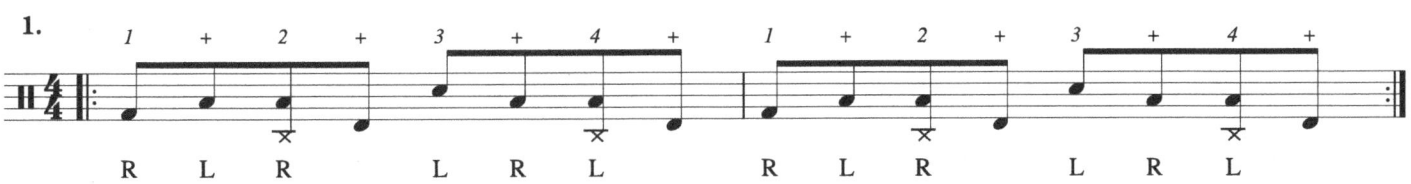

Floor tom and tom-tom share the last beat of the phrase:

Combination with toms; with bass drum on *4*:

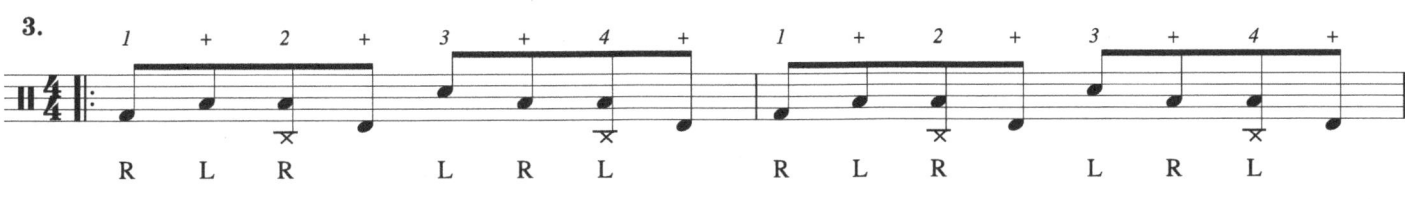

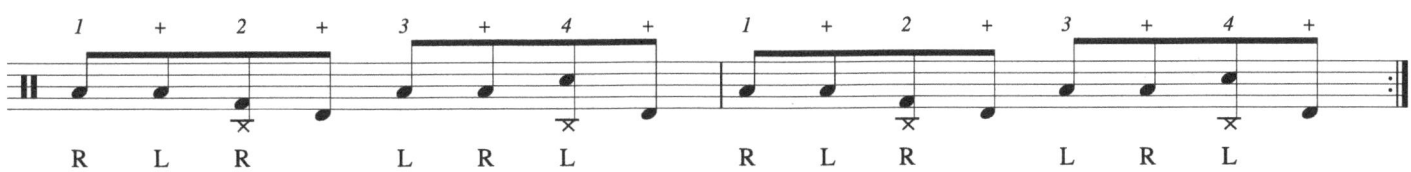

Reverse application:

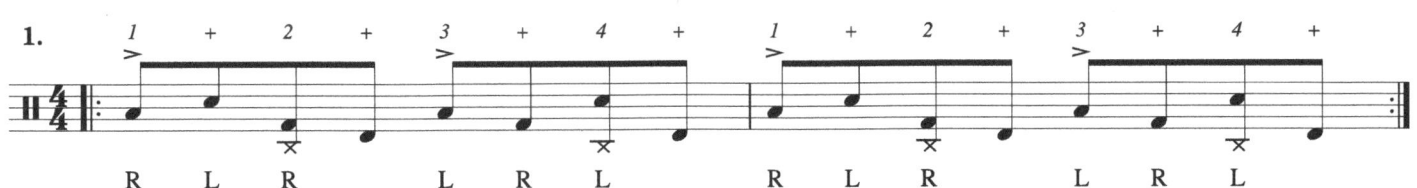

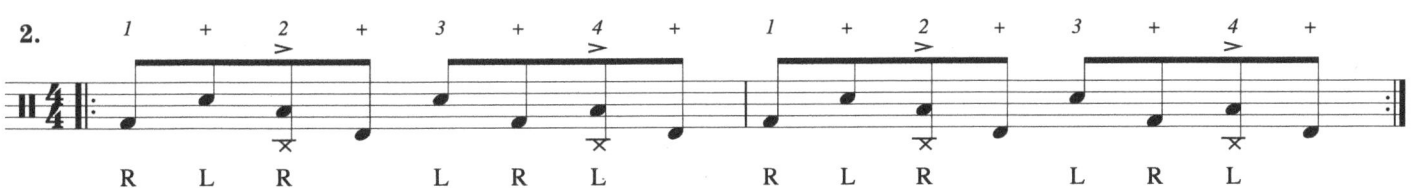

23

Combine 1 & 2:

LESSON 15
The Three-Stroke Ruff

Separate hands; develop equal and balanced tonality.

Separate hands, floor tom and snare drum:

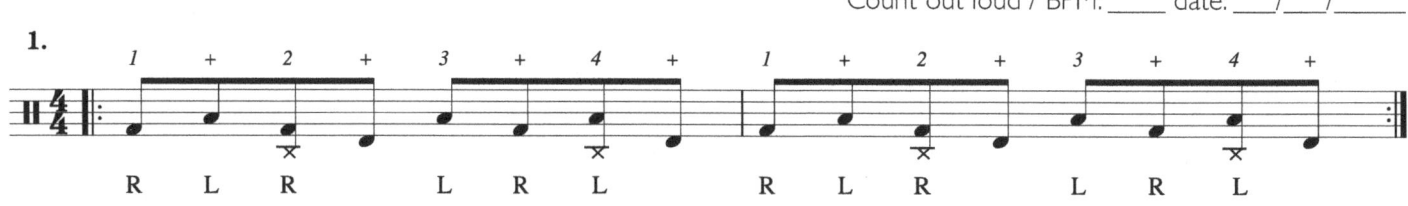

Separate hands, snare drum and tom-tom:

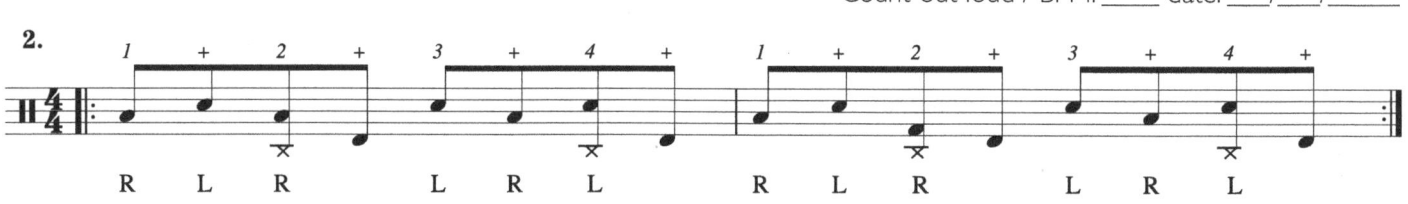

Separate hands, floor tom and tom-tom:

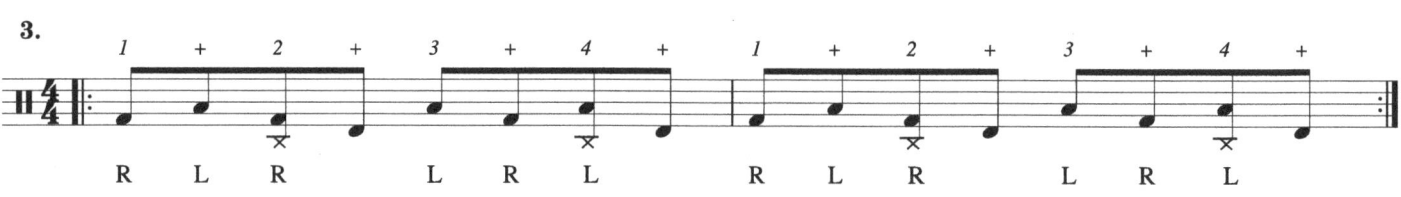

Combine:

LESSON 16
The Three-Stroke Ruff Around the Kit

Snare drum, tom-tom and floor tom; move clockwise around the kit:

Count out loud / BPM: ____ date: ___/___/____

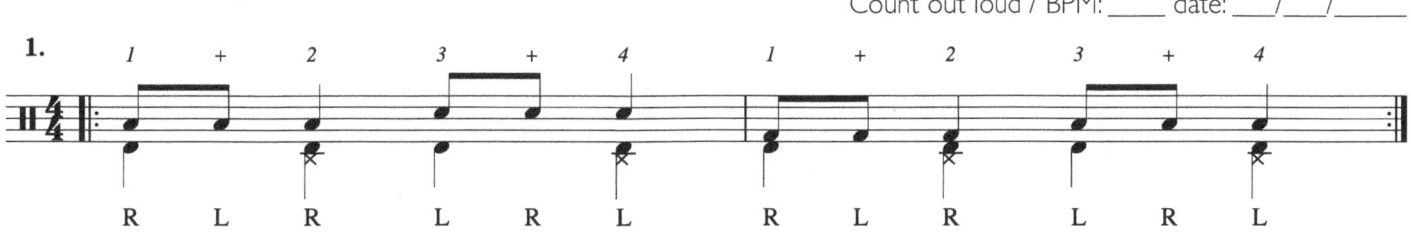

Move counterclockwise around the kit:

Count out loud / BPM: ____ date: ___/___/____

Floor tom, tom-tom and snare drum:

Count out loud / BPM: ____ date: ___/___/____

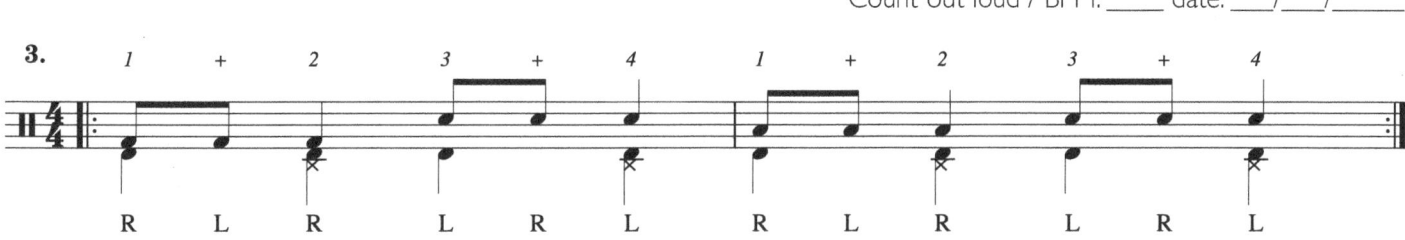

LESSON 17
The Three-Stroke Ruff

Combine three different downbeats with rim shots (>). Rim shots must be hit lightly in order to gain clarity and speed.

Count out loud / BPM: ____ date: ___/___/____

25

LESSON 18
The Three-Stroke Ruff

Wrist and bass drum exercises. Try not to run over your bass drum with the flexibility (speed) of your hands.

Count out loud / BPM: ____ date: ___/___/____

Exchange alternating strokes with bass drum:

Count out loud / BPM: ____ date: ___/___/____

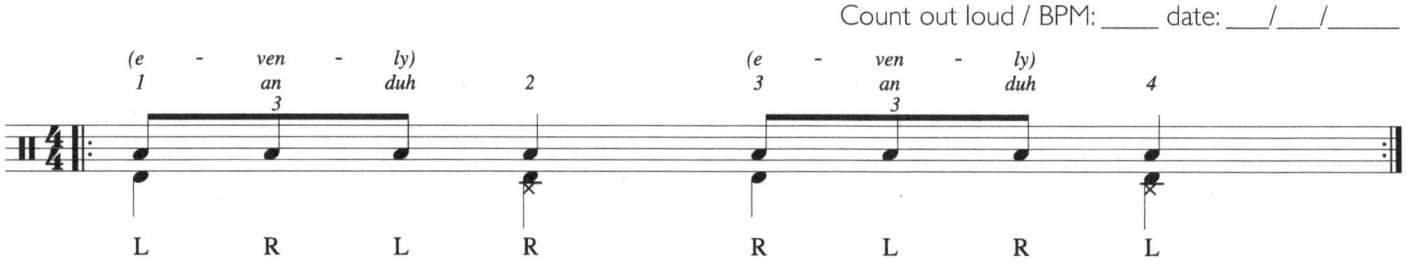

LESSON 19
The Four-Stroke Ruff

Bass drum on the first beat and last beat of the phrase. Subdivide bass drum with hi-hat.

Rhythmic model:

Count out loud / BPM: ____ date: ___/___/____

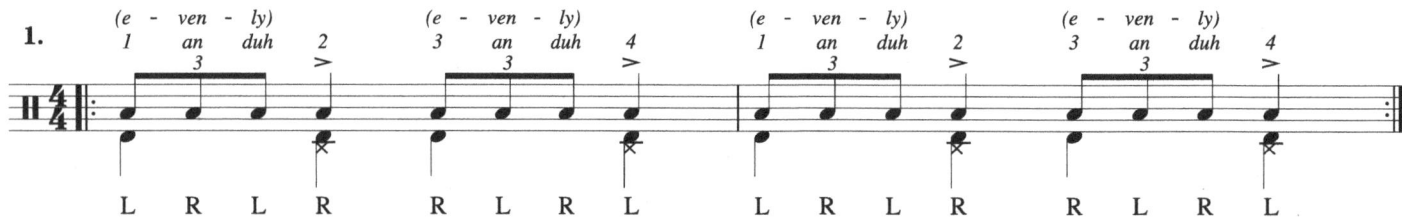

With accents on end of phrase:

Count out loud / BPM: ____ date: ___/___/____

With accents on beginning of phrase:

Count out loud / BPM: ____ date: ___/___/____

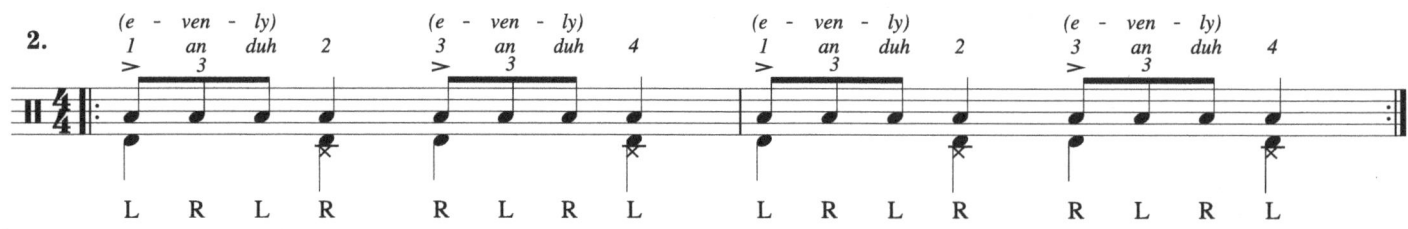

Combine 1 & 2:

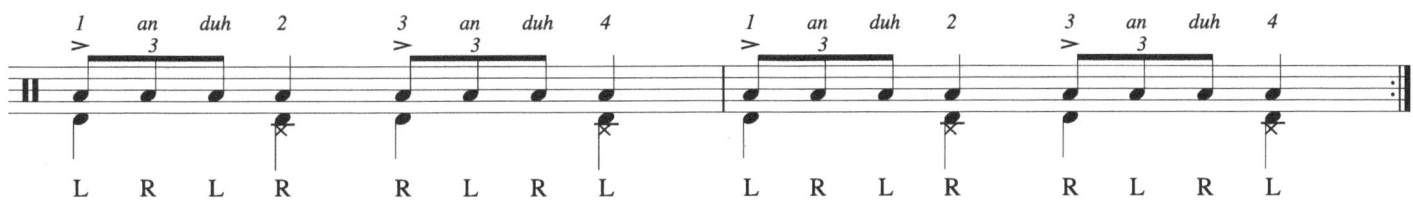

LESSON 20
The Four-Stroke Ruff

Substitute toms in place of accents.

With toms on end of phrase:

With toms on beginning of phrase:

Combine 1 & 2:

Count out loud / BPM: _____ date: ___/___/_____

Reverse application:

Count out loud / BPM: _____ date: ___/___/_____

Count out loud / BPM: _____ date: ___/___/_____

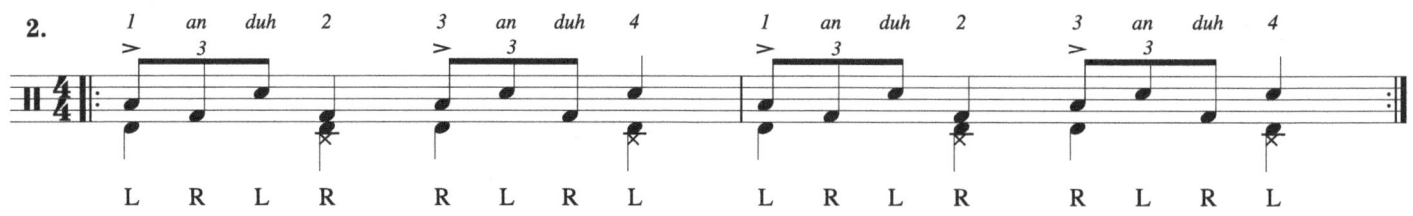

Combine 1 & 2:

Count out loud / BPM: _____ date: ___/___/_____

LESSON 21
The Four-Stroke Ruff

Separating hands, with one hand per drum. Listen for double-stroke pattern within the ruff.

Snare drum and floor tom:

Count out loud / BPM: ____ date: ___/___/___

Tom-tom and snare drum:

Count out loud / BPM: ____ date: ___/___/___

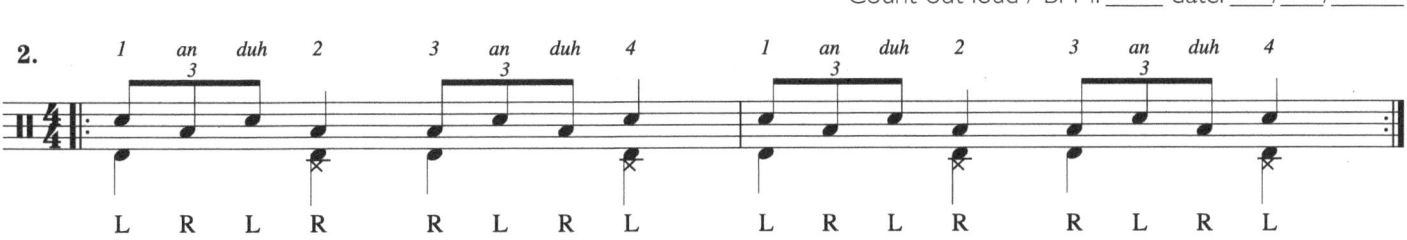

Tom and floor tom:

Count out loud / BPM: ____ date: ___/___/___

Combinations:

Count out loud / BPM: ____ date: ___/___/___

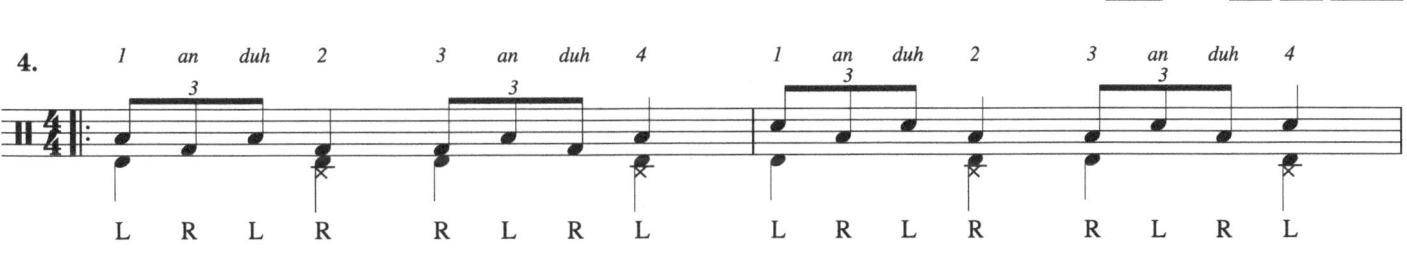

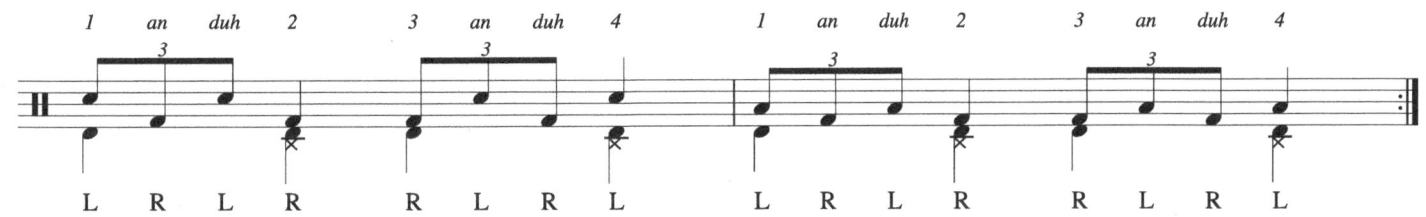

LESSON 22
The Four-Stroke Ruff

Feather bass drum; accent bass drum on cymbal crashes.

With crash cymbals and bass drum on last beat of phrase:

With crash cymbals and bass drum on first beat of phrase:

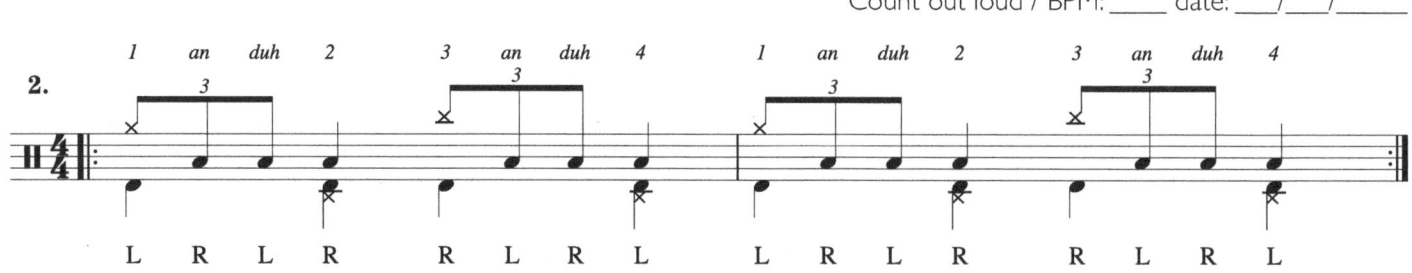

Combine both exercises:

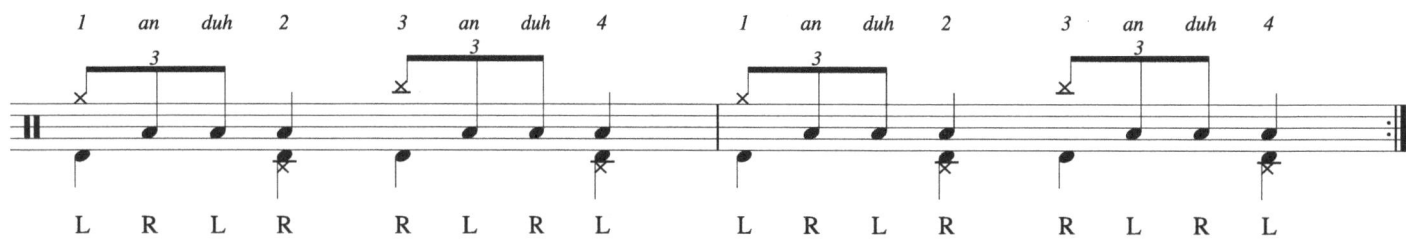

LESSON 23
The Four-Stroke Ruff

With bass drum on fifth beat, be sure to secure heel & toe with hi-hat. Accents will pop with the feet secured in the downbeat; then substitute toms for accented strokes.

Rhythmic model:

Count out loud / BPM: _____ date: ___/___/_____

Add accents on last beat of phrase:

Count out loud / BPM: _____ date: ___/___/_____

1.

Add accents on first beat of phrase:

Count out loud / BPM: _____ date: ___/___/_____

2.

Combination of accents:

Count out loud / BPM: _____ date: ___/___/_____

3.

LESSON 24
The Four-Stroke Ruff

With bass drum on the sixth beat. After developing the accent, deliver the accented strokes to the toms and then to the cymbals.

Rhythmic model:

With accents on last beat of phrase:

With accents on first beat of phrase:

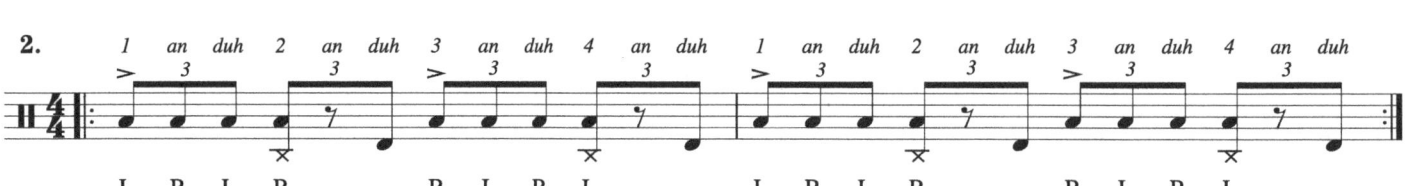

Combination of accents:

LESSON 25
The Four-Stroke Ruff

With bass drum on *5* and *6*. After developing the accents, deliver the accented strokes to the toms and then to the crash cymbals.

Rhythmic model:

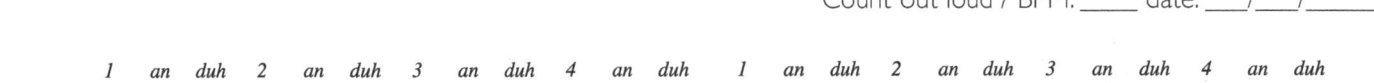

Add accents on last beat of phrase:

Add accents to first beat of phrase:

Combination of accents:

LESSON 26
The Four-Stroke Ruff Around the Kit

These are hand-to-hand exercises around the kit.

Move clockwise around the kit:

Count out loud / BPM: ____ date: ___/___/___

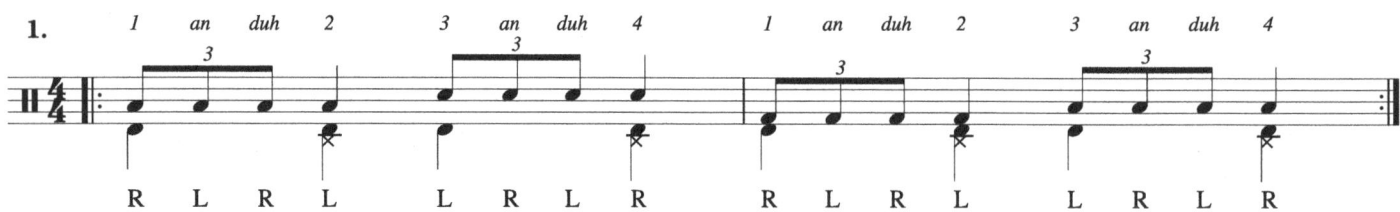

Move counterclockwise around the kit:

Count out loud / BPM: ____ date: ___/___/___

LESSON 27
The Four-Stroke Ruff Wrist and Bass Drum Exercises

Count out loud / BPM: ____ date: ___/___/___

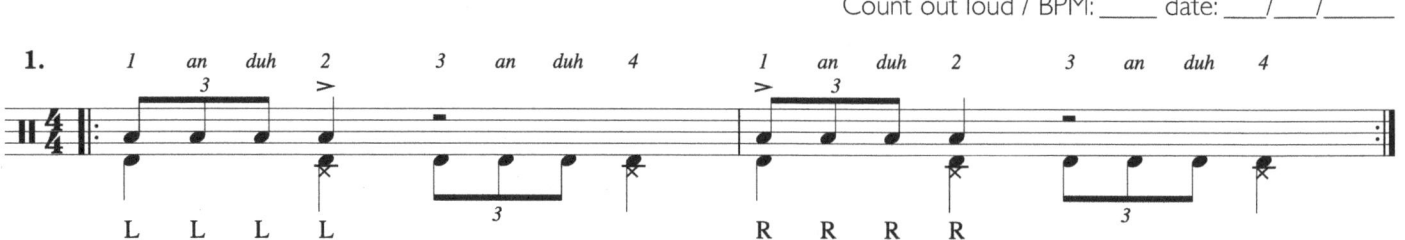

Exchange alternating strokes with bass drum:

Count out loud / BPM: ____ date: ___/___/___

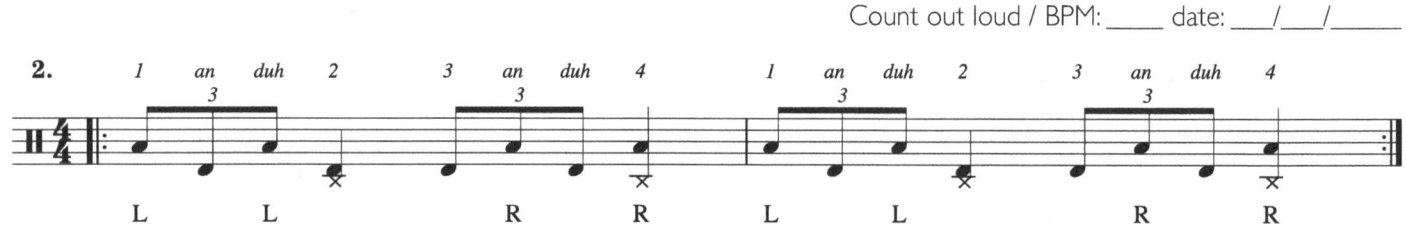

LESSON 28
The Five-Stroke Ruff

Bass drum is on every other beat of the phrase.
Subdivide the bass drum with the hi-hat.

Rhythmic model:

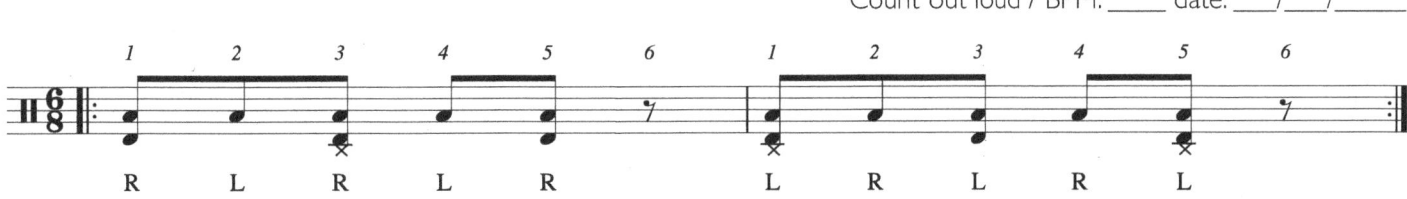

With accent on last beat of phrase:

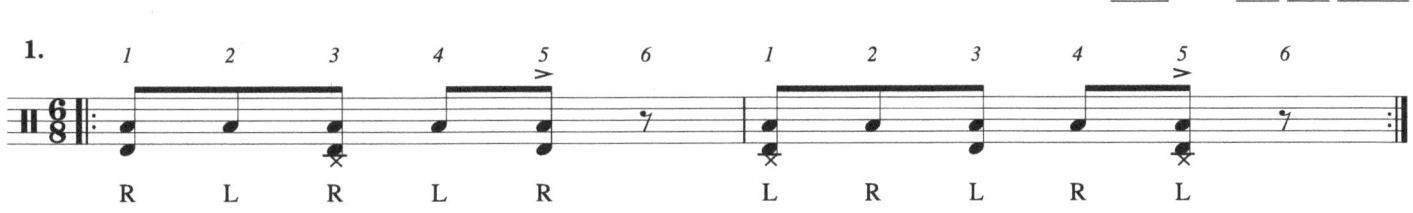

With accent on first beat of phrase:

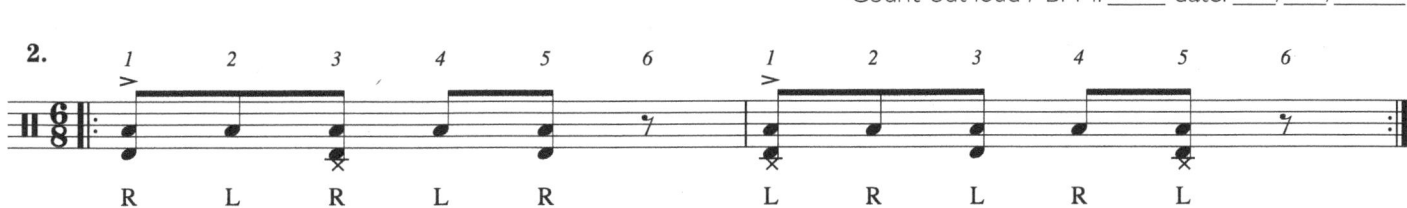

Combination of accents:

LESSON 29
The Five-Stroke Ruff

Substitute toms in place of accents.

With tom on end of phrase:

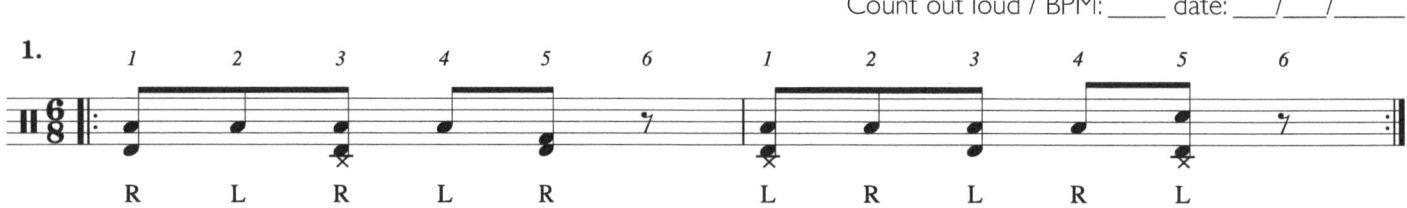

With toms on beginning of phrase:

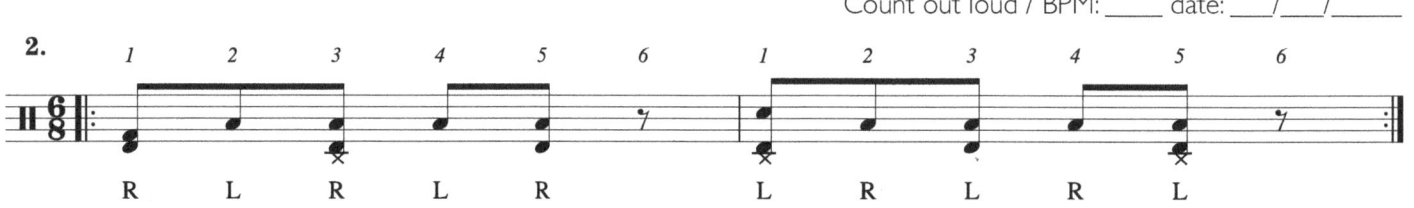

Combine 1 & 2:

Reverse application:

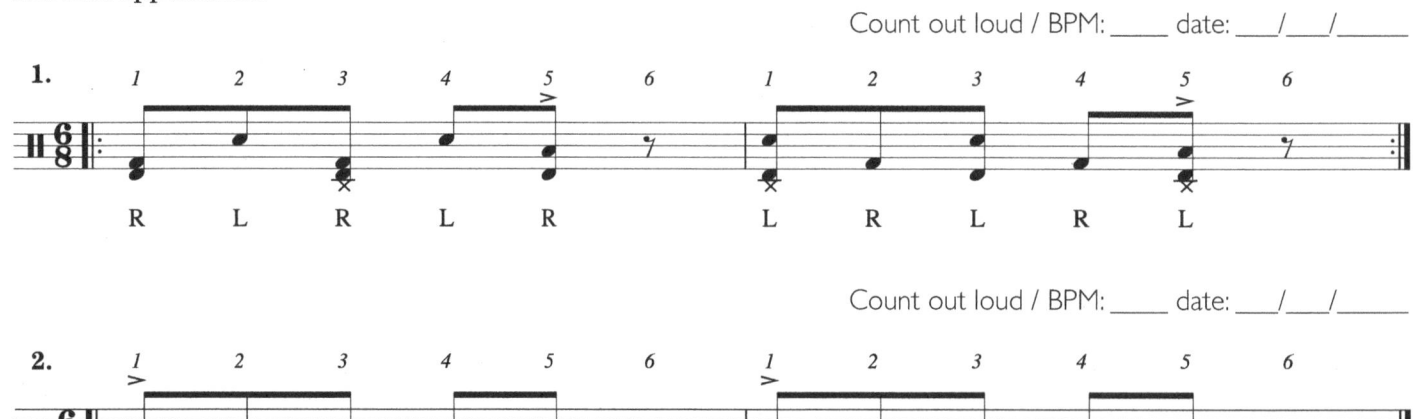

Combine 1 & 2:

Count out loud / BPM: ____ date: ___/___/_____

LESSON 30
The Five-Stroke Ruff

Separating hands, with one hand per drum.

Floor tom and snare drum:

Count out loud / BPM: ____ date: ___/___/_____

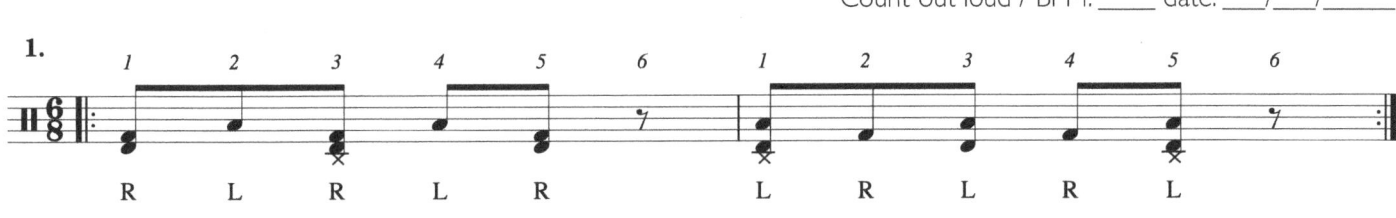

Snare drum and tom-tom:

Count out loud / BPM: ____ date: ___/___/_____

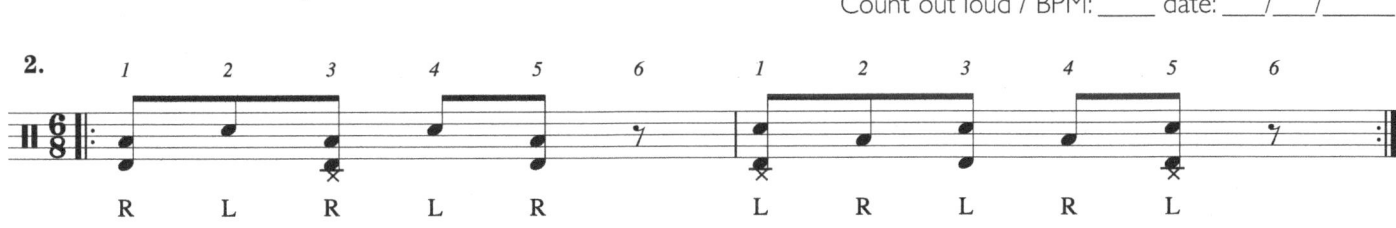

Floor tom and tom-tom:

Count out loud / BPM: ____ date: ___/___/_____

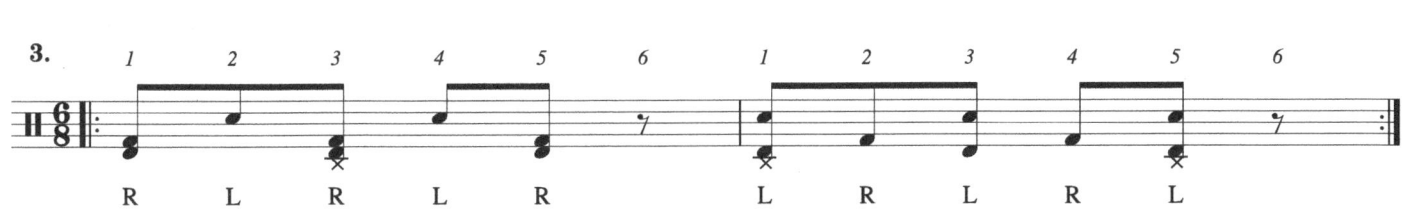

Combinations:

Count out loud / BPM: ____ date: ___/___/____

LESSON 31
The Five-Stroke Ruff

With crash cymbals on the last beat of the phrase and on the first beat of the phrase. Feather the bass drum, accenting on cymbal crashes.

With crash cymbals and bass drum on last beat of phrase:

Count out loud / BPM: ____ date: ___/___/____

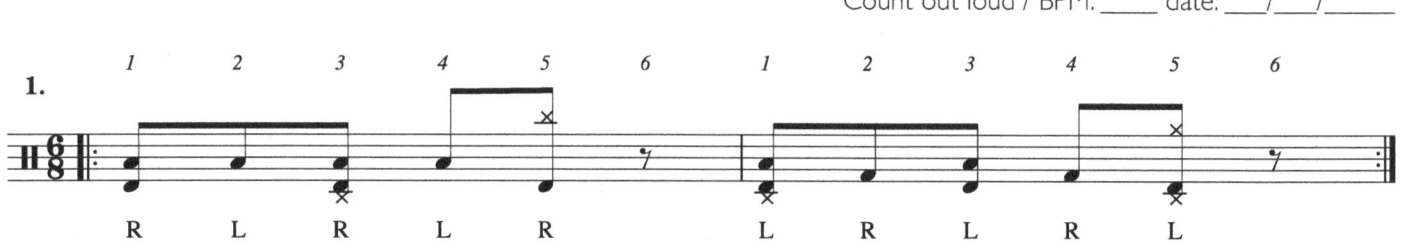

With crash cymbals and bass drum on first beat of phrase:

Count out loud / BPM: ____ date: ___/___/____

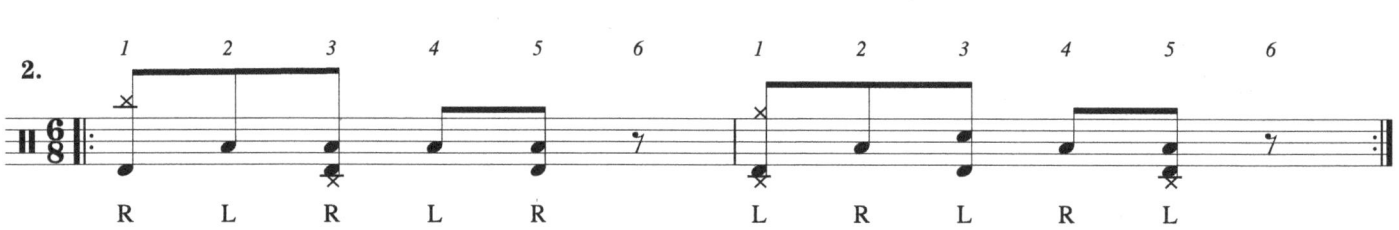

Combine both exercises:

Count out loud / BPM: ____ date: ___/___/____

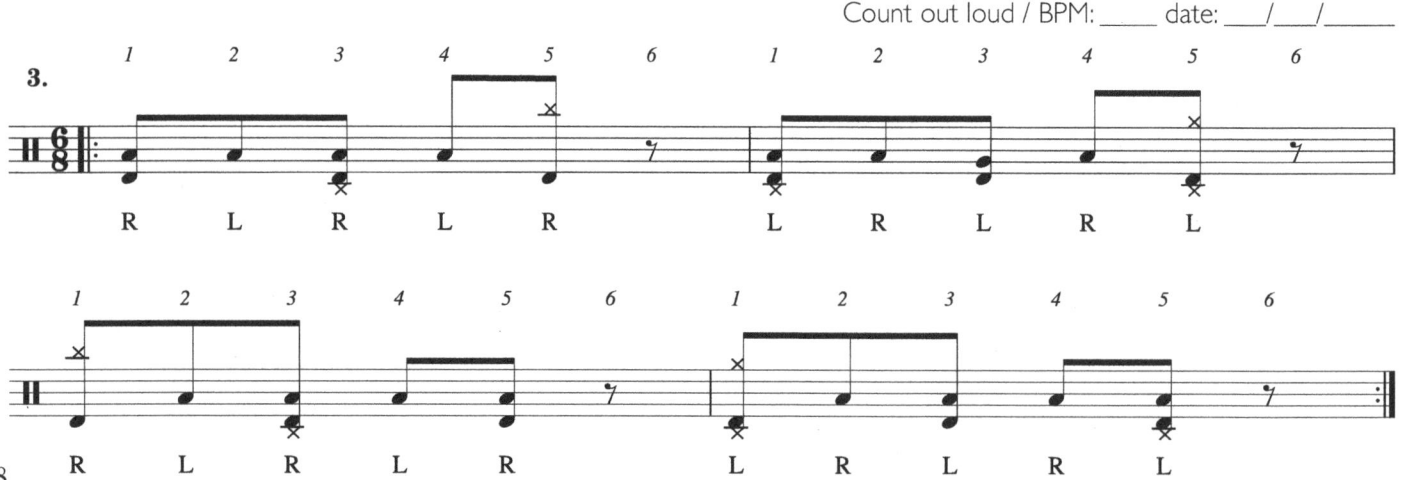

LESSON 32
The Five-Stroke Ruff

With bass drum on sixth beat. After developing accents, deliver the accented strokes to the toms and cymbals.

Rhythmic model:

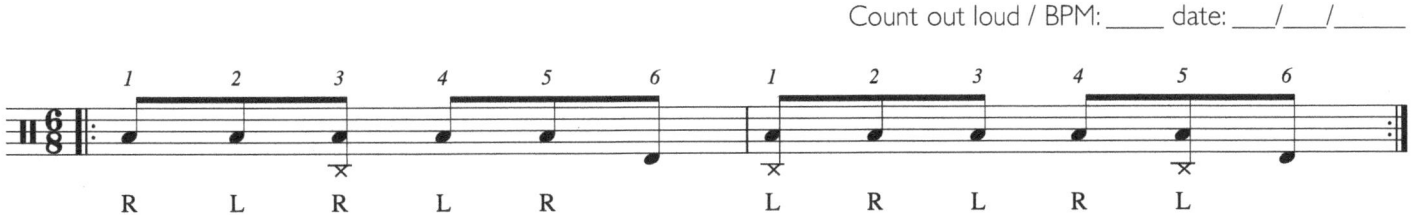

Add accents to last beat of phrase:

Add accents to first beat of phrase:

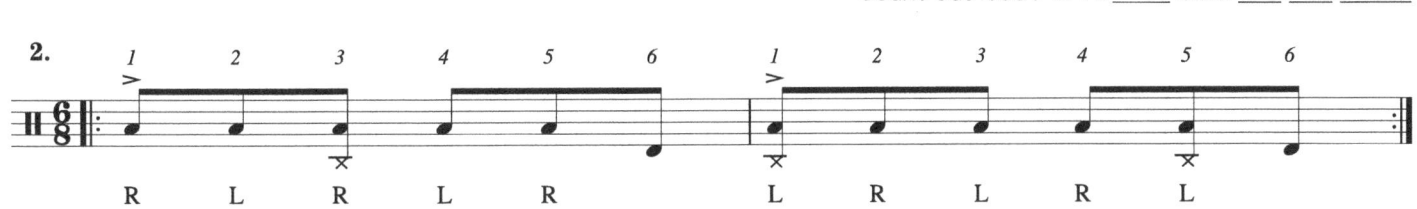

Combinations of accents:

LESSON 33
The Five-Stroke Ruff

With bass drum on sixth beat. Substitute accents with tom-toms.

Toms on last stroke:

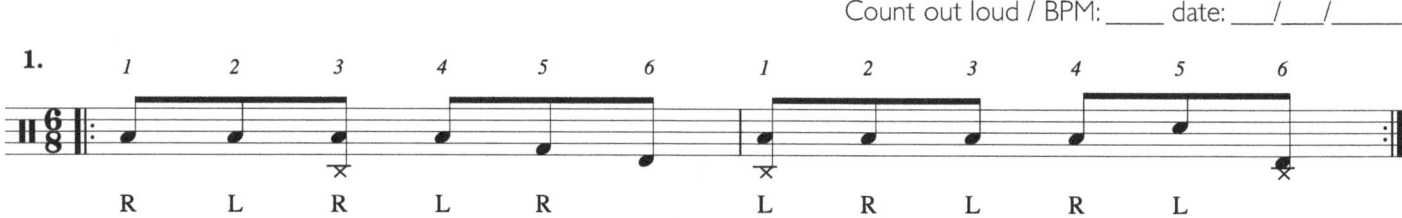

Toms on first beat:

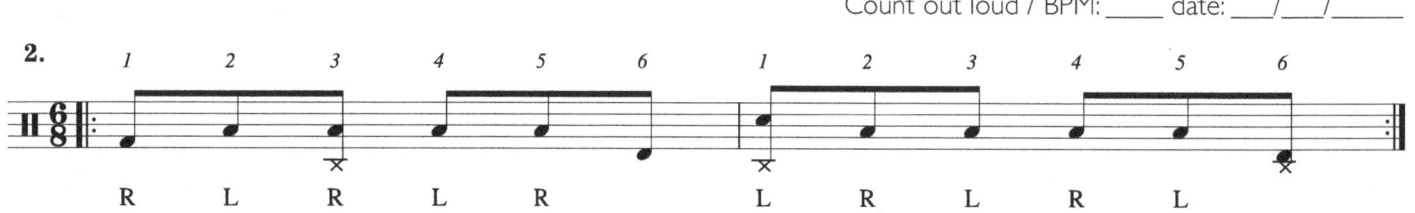

Combinations with toms; bass drum on *6*:

Reverse application, with snare drum receiving accented stroke substitution on last stroke of phrase:

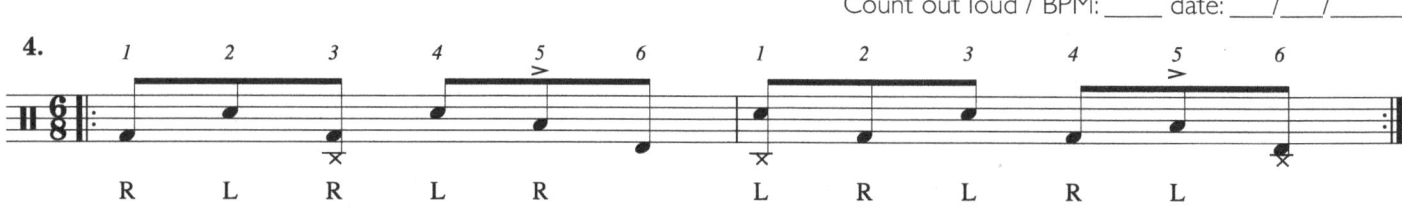

With snare drum accented stroke substitution on first beat of phrase:

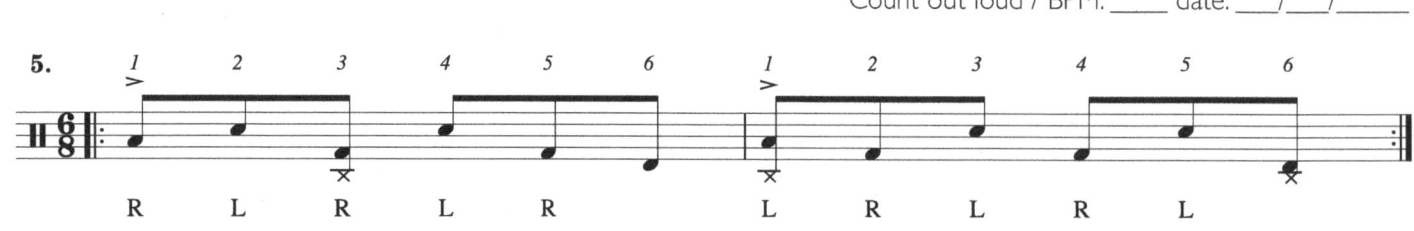

Combine:

Count out loud / BPM: _____ date: ___/___/_____

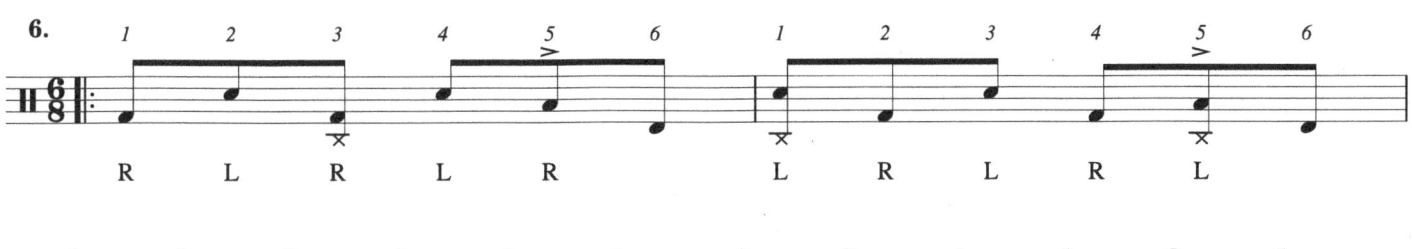

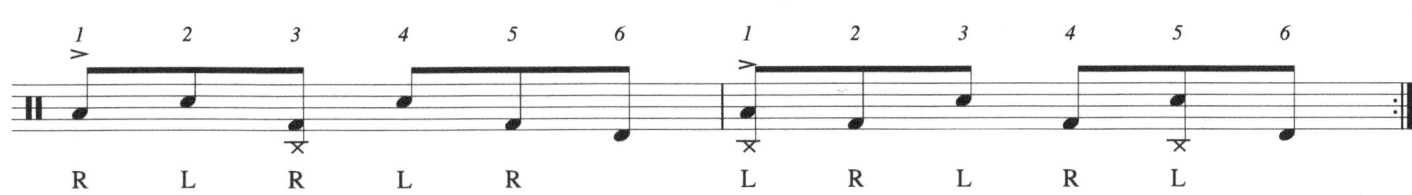

LESSON 34
The Five-Stroke Ruff

With bass drum on the sixth beat, separate hands.

Separate hands, floor tom and snare drum:

Count out loud / BPM: _____ date: ___/___/_____

Separate hands, snare drum and tom-tom:

Count out loud / BPM: _____ date: ___/___/_____

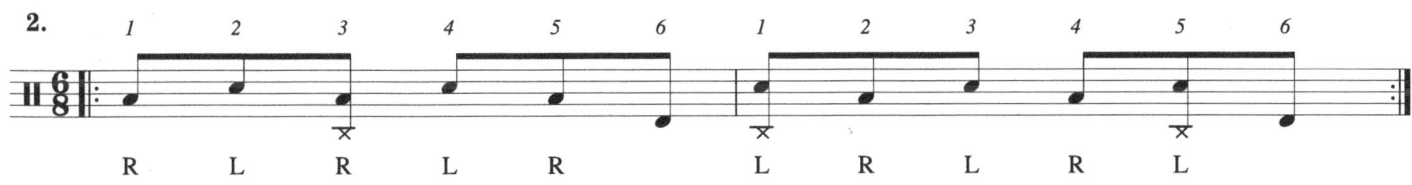

Separate hands, floor tom and tom-tom:

Count out loud / BPM: _____ date: ___/___/_____

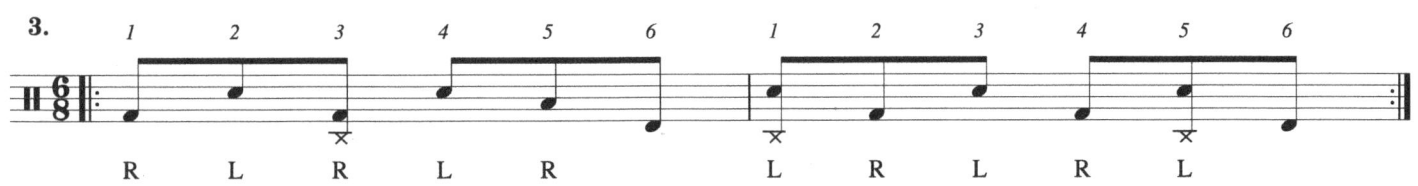

Combine:

LESSON 35
The Five-Stroke Ruff Around the Kit

Hand-to-hand exercise using three drums.

Move clockwise around the kit:

Move counterclockwise around the kit:

Floor tom, snare drum and tom-tom:

LESSON 36
The Five-Stroke Roll

Bass drum is on every other beat. Hi-hat subdivides the bass drum.

Rhythmic model:

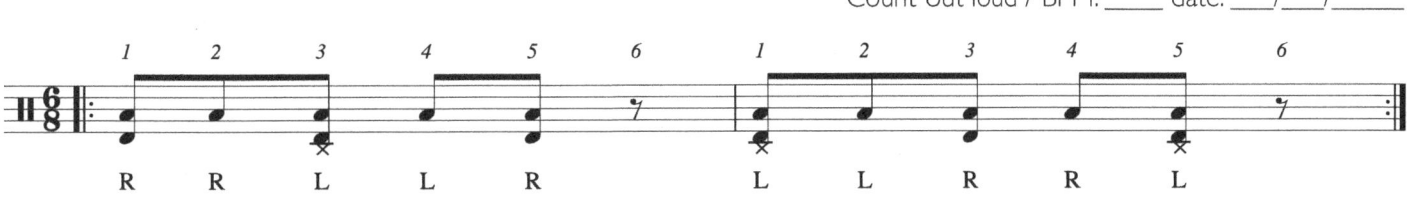

With accent on last beat of phrase:

With the accent on first beat of phrase:

Combination of accents:

LESSON 37
The Five-Stroke Roll

Substitute toms in place of accents.

With tom at end of phrase:

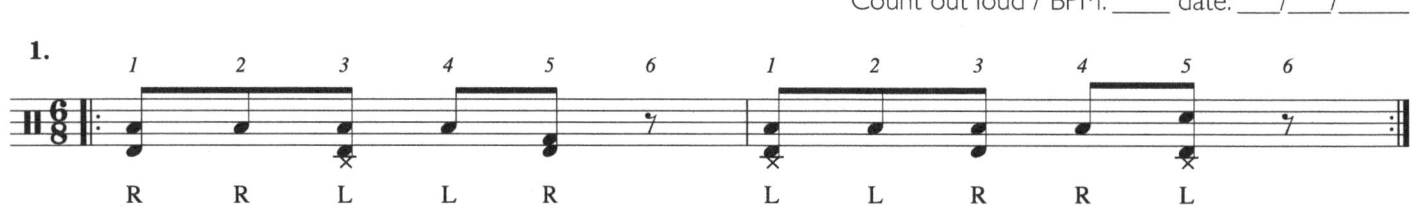

Reverse, with snare at end of phrase:

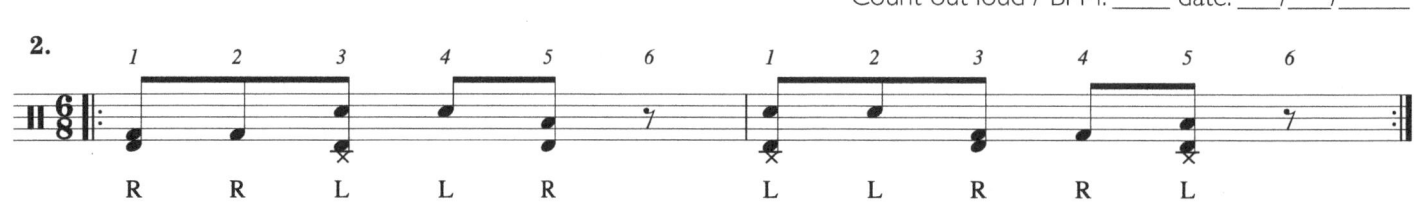

Combine 1 & 2:

LESSON 38
The Five-Stroke Roll

Separate hands, one hand per drum.

Floor tom and snare drum:

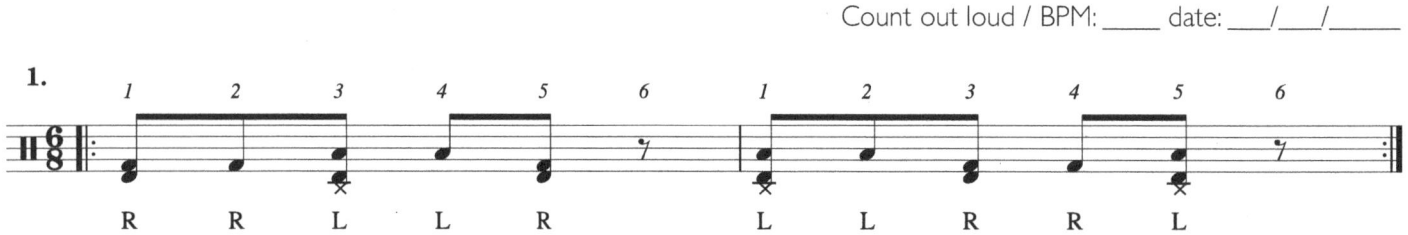

44

Snare drum and tom-tom:

Floor tom and tom-tom:

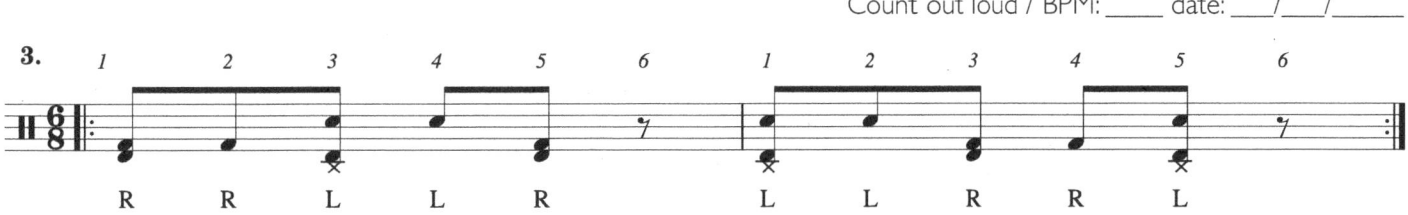

Combinations:

LESSON 39
The Five-Stroke Roll

With crash cymbals on last beat of phrase, feather the bass drum, accenting on cymbal crashes.

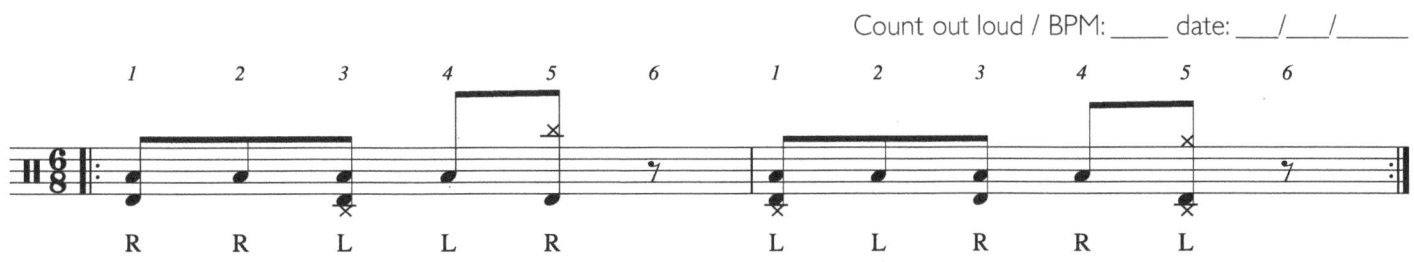

LESSON 40
The Five-Stroke Roll

With bass drum on the sixth beat.

Rhythmic model:

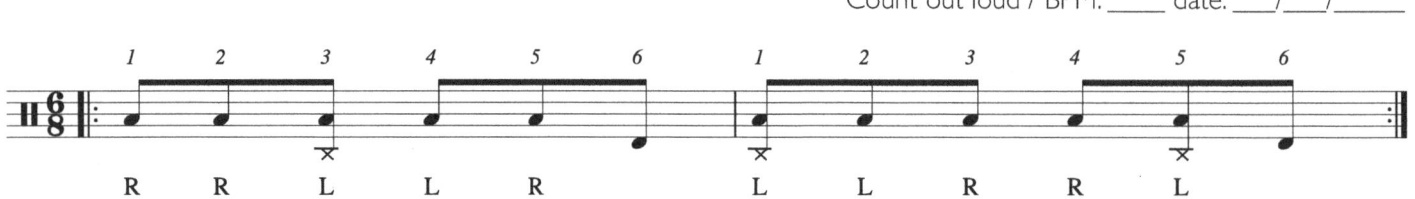

Accent on last beat of phrase:

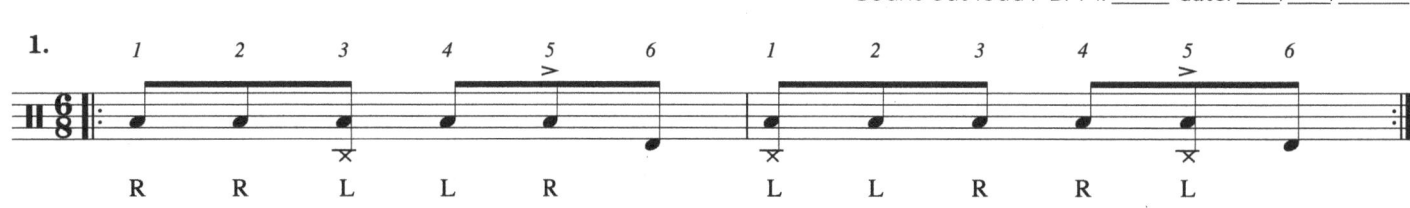

Accent on first beat of phrase:

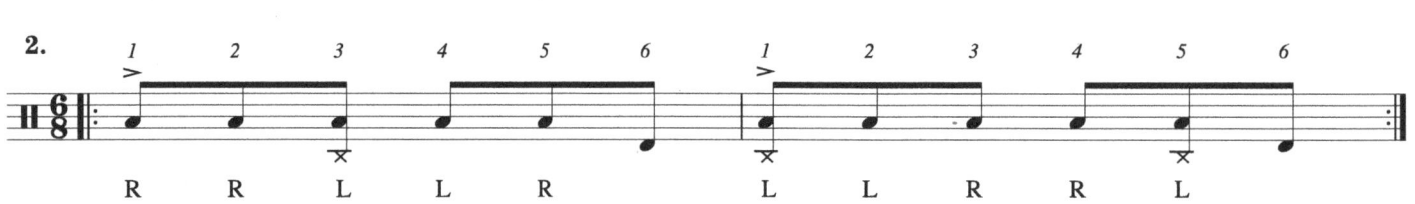

Combine accented phrases:

LESSON 41
The Five-Stroke Roll

With bass drum on the sixth beat, substitute accents with toms.

With toms on end of phrase:

Reverse, with snare drum on end of phrase:

Combinations with bass drum on *6*:

LESSON 42
The Five-Stroke Roll

With bass drum on the sixth beat, separate hands.

Separate hands, floor tom and snare drum:

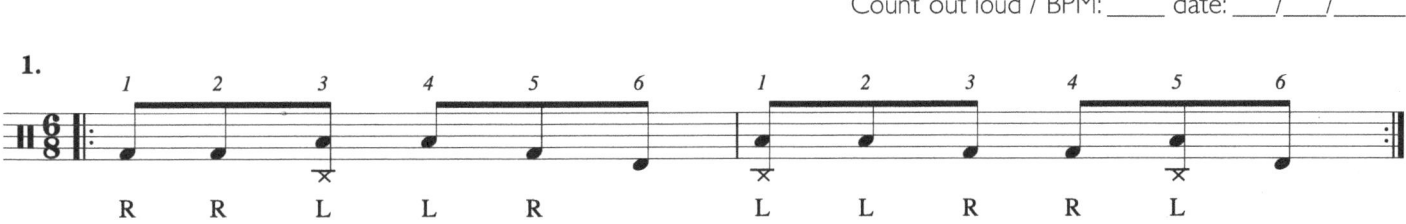

Separate hands, snare drum and tom-tom:

Separate hands, tom-tom and floor tom:

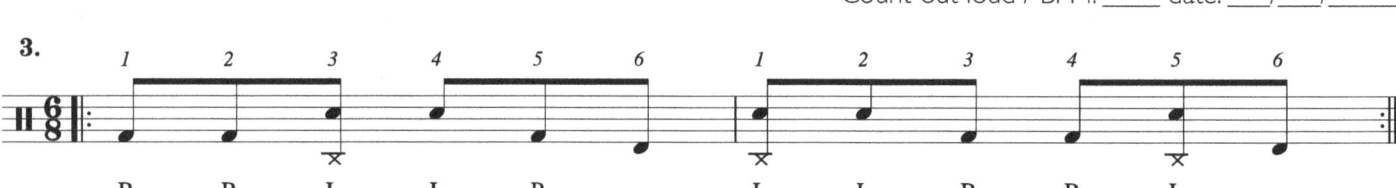

Combine:

LESSON 43
The Five-Stroke Roll Around the Kit

Three drums, five strokes per drum.

Snare drum, tom-tom and floor tom; move clockwise around the kit:

Snare drum, floor tom and tom-tom; counterclockwise:

Floor tom, snare drum and tom-tom:

LESSON 44
Wrist Exercises for the Five-Stroke Roll and Ruff

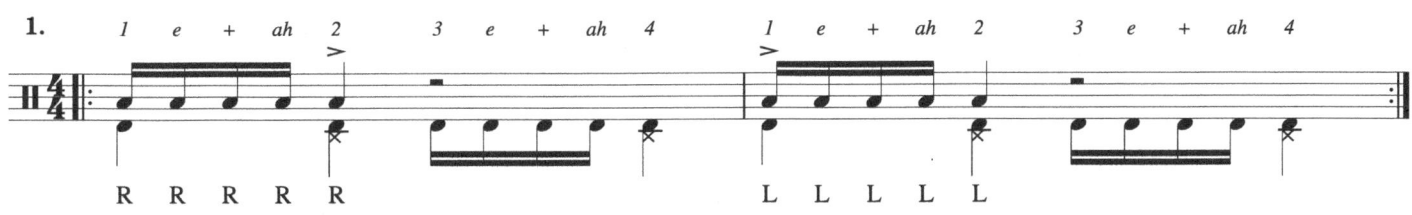

Exchange alternating strokes with bass drum and snare drum:

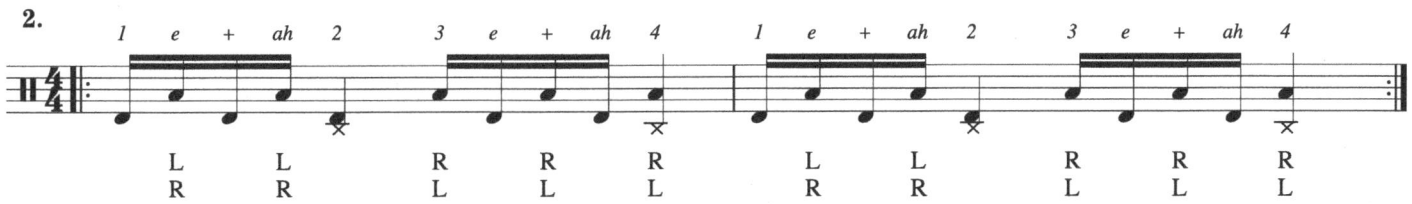

LESSON 45
The Seven-Stroke Ruff

Bass drum on every other beat of the phrase. Subdivide bass drum with hi-hat.

Rhythmic model:

With accents on end of phrase:

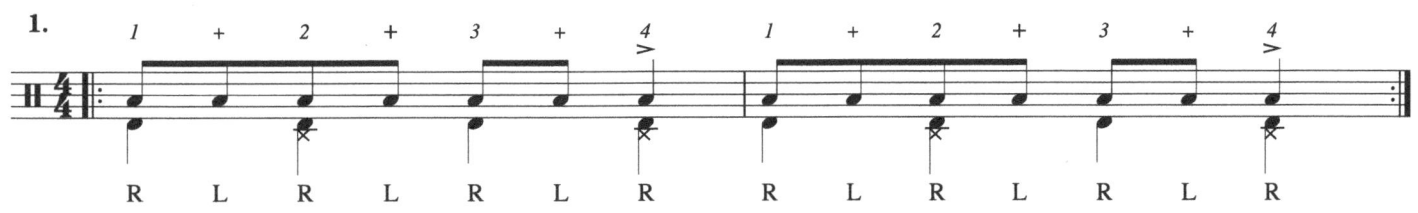

With accents on beginning of phrase:

Combine 1 & 2:

LESSON 46
The Seven-Stroke Ruff

Substitute toms in place of accents.

With toms on end of phrase:

With toms on beginning of phrase:

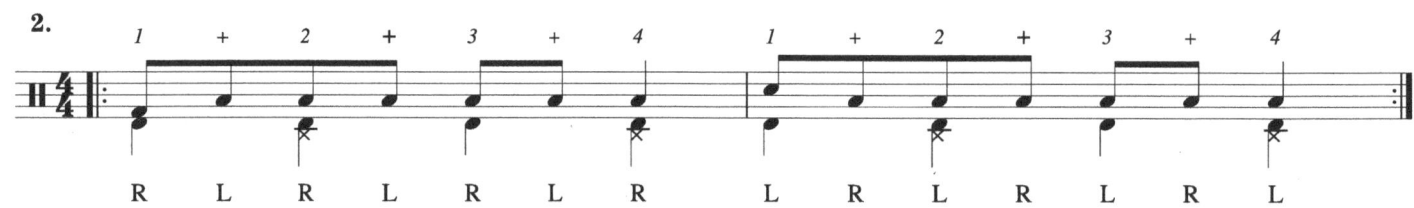

Combine 1 & 2:

Reverse application:

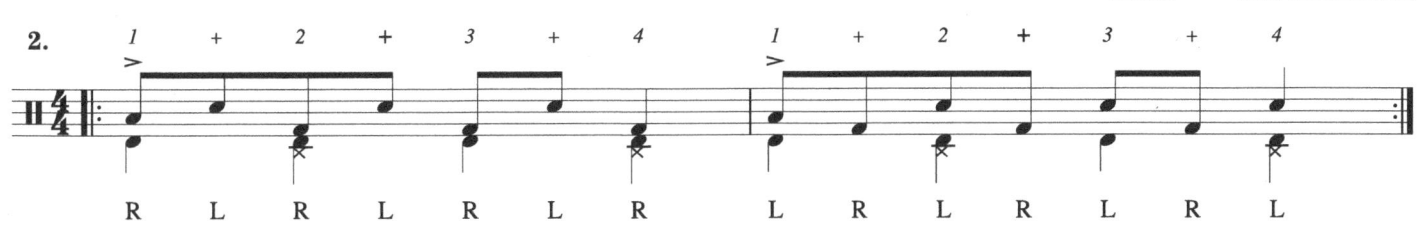

Combine 1 & 2:

LESSON 47
The Seven-Stroke Ruff

Separate hands, one hand per drum.

Floor tom and snare drum:

Count out loud / BPM: ____ date: ___/___/____

Snare drum and tom:

Count out loud / BPM: ____ date: ___/___/____

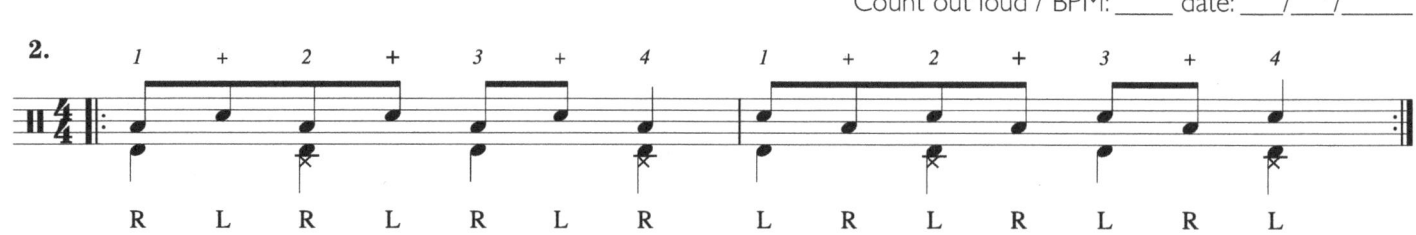

Floor tom and tom-tom:

Count out loud / BPM: ____ date: ___/___/____

Combinations:

Count out loud / BPM: ____ date: ___/___/____

LESSON 48
The Seven-Stroke Ruff

With crash cymbals on last and first beats of the phrase.
Feather the bass drum, accenting on cymbal crashes.

With crash cymbals and bass drum on last beat:

With crash cymbals and bass drum on first beat of phrase:

Combine 1 & 2:

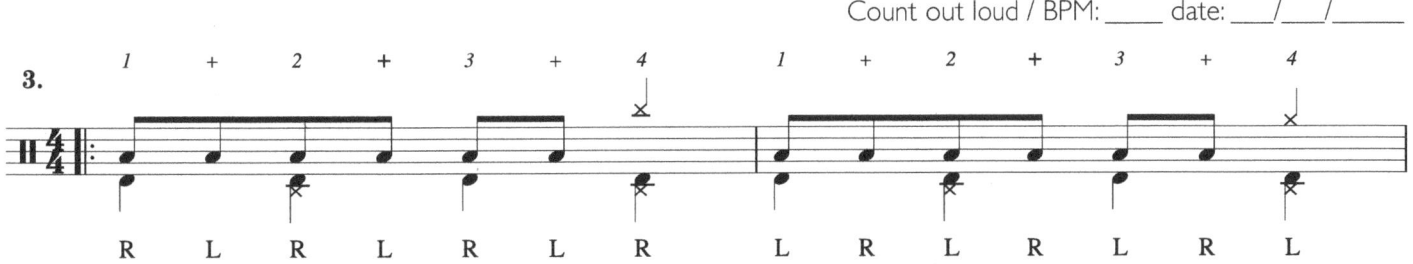

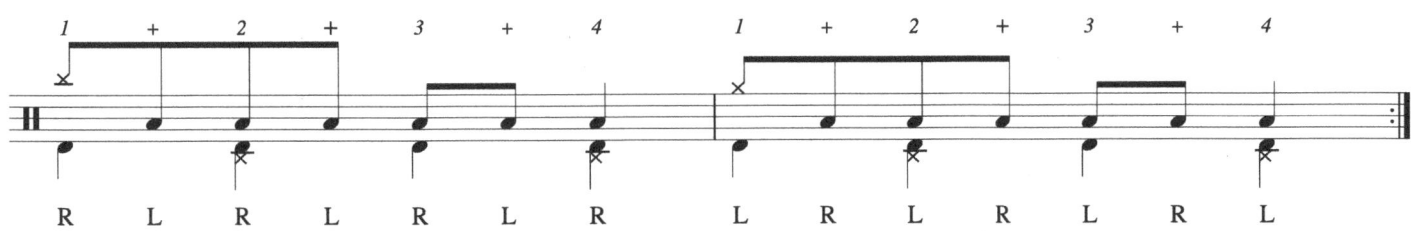

53

LESSON 49
The Seven-Stroke Ruff

With bass drum on the *and* of *4*. After developing the accents, deliver the accented strokes to the toms and cymbals.

Rhythmic model:

Add accents on last beat of phrase:

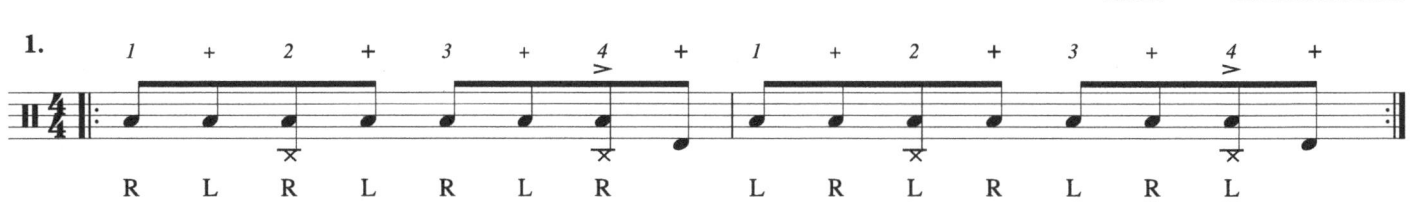

Add accents on first beat of phrase:

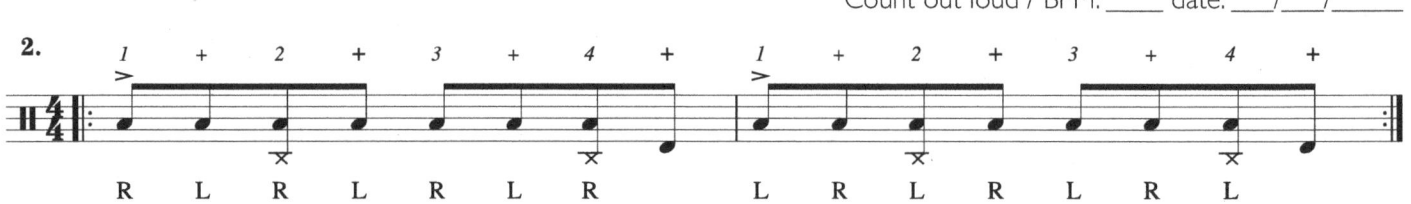

Combination of accents:

LESSON 50
The Seven-Stroke Ruff Around the Kit

Hand-to-hand exercises around the kit.

Move clockwise around the kit:

Move counterclockwise around the kit:

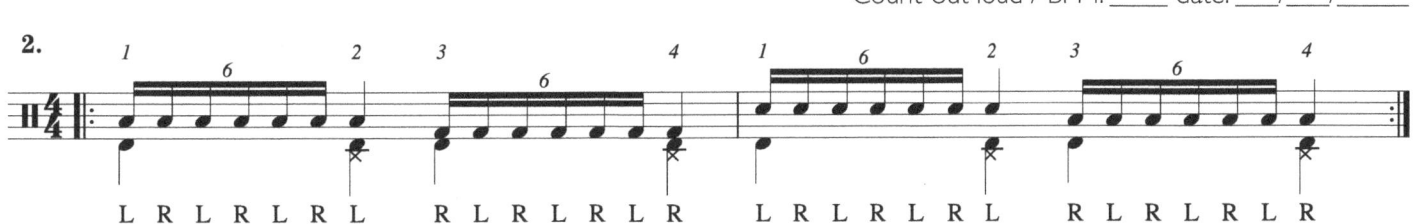

LESSON 51
The Seven-Stroke Roll

Bass drum on every other beat.

Rhythmic model:

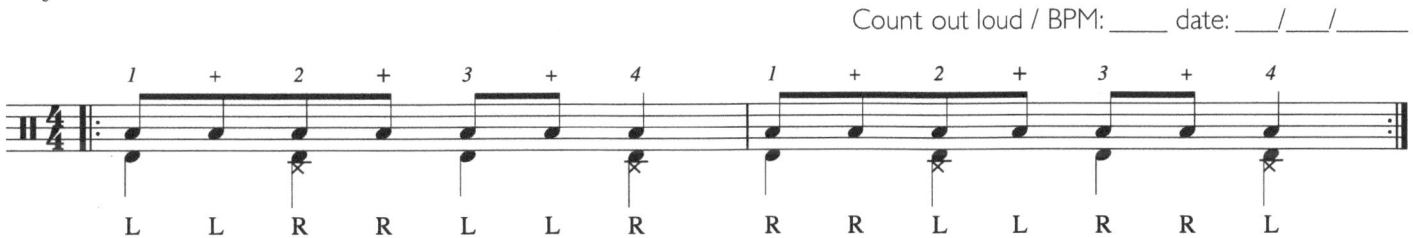

With accents on end of phrase:

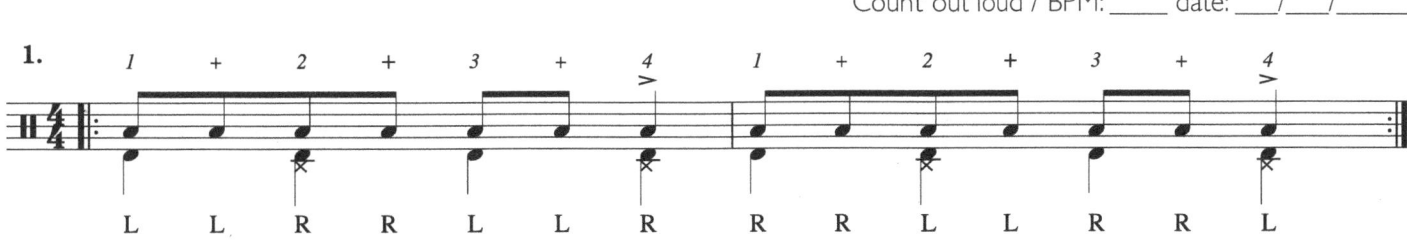

With accents on beginning of phrase:

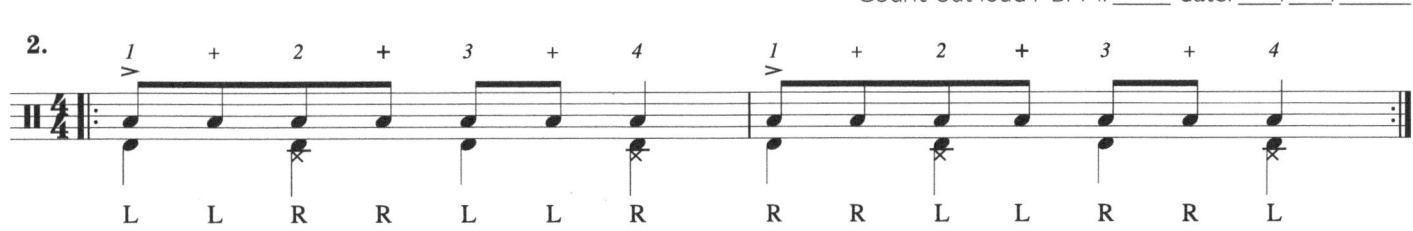

Combine 1 & 2:

LESSON 52
The Seven-Stroke Roll

Tom and snare placement.

With toms on end of phrase:

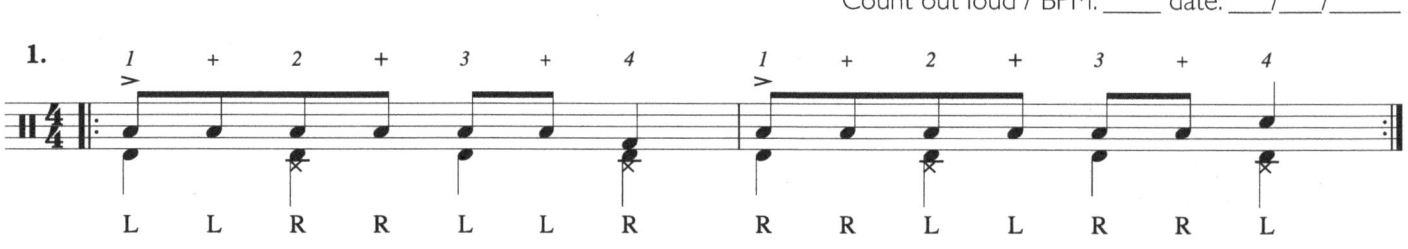

Reverse, with snare on beginning of phrase:

Combine 1 & 2:

LESSON 53
The Seven-Stroke Roll

Seven strokes per drum.

Clockwise:

Counterclockwise:

LESSON 54
The Seven-Stroke Roll

With bass drum on the *and* of *4*.

Rhythmic model:

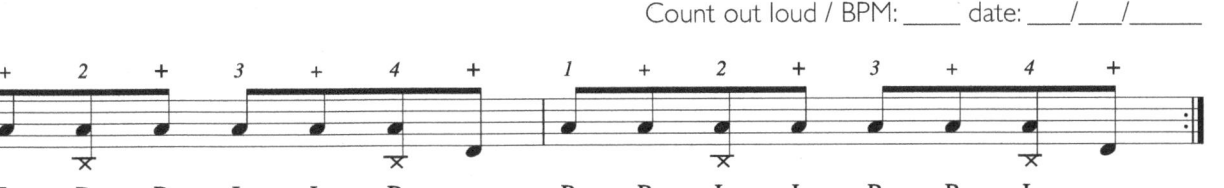

With accents on last beat of phrase:

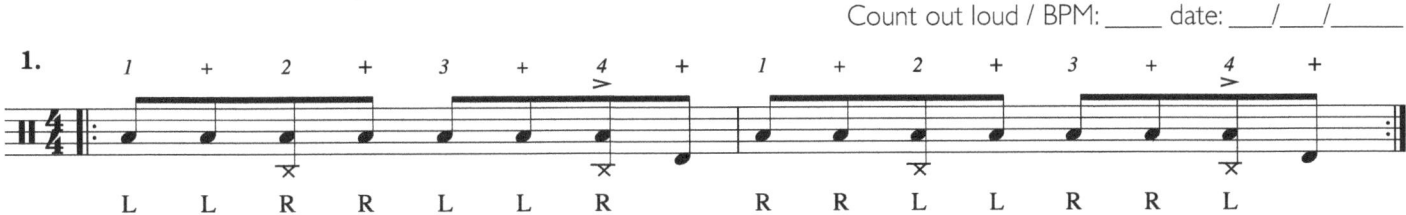

With accents on first beat of phrase:

Combine accented phrases:

Count out loud / BPM: ____ date: ___/___/_____

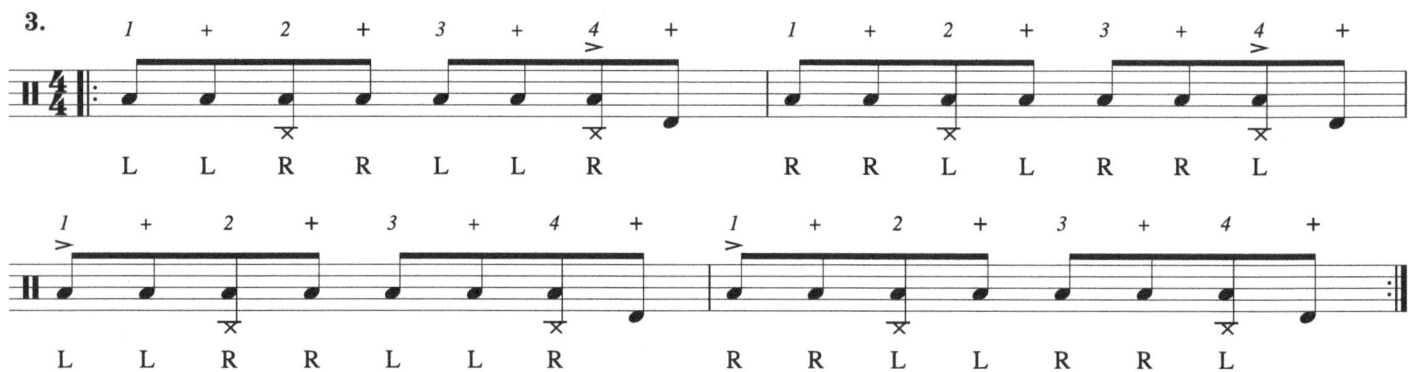

LESSON 55
The Seven-Stroke Roll

With bass drum on the *and* of 4, substitute tom on downbeat of 4.

With toms on end of phrase:

Count out loud / BPM: ____ date: ___/___/_____

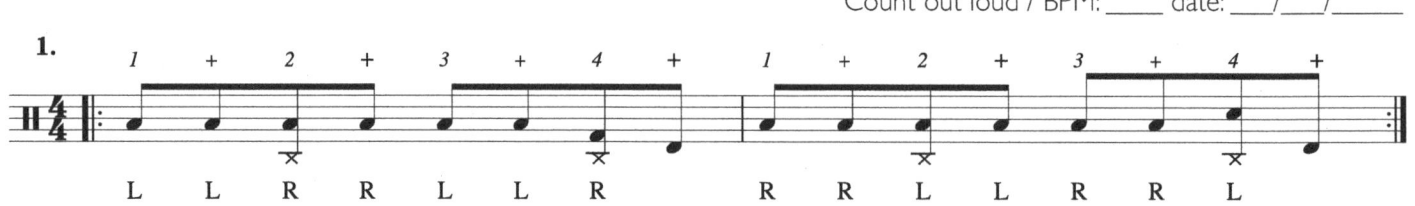

Reverse, with snare on end of phrase:

Count out loud / BPM: ____ date: ___/___/_____

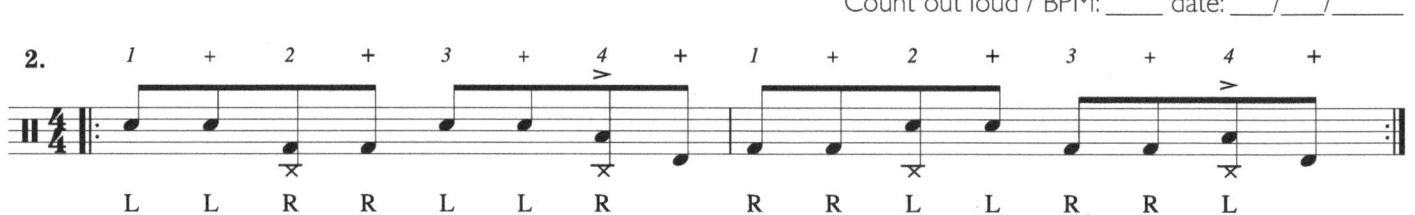

LESSON 56
The Seven-Stroke Roll

With bass drum on the *and* of 4, separate hands.

Snare drum and floor tom:

Count out loud / BPM: ____ date: ___/___/_____

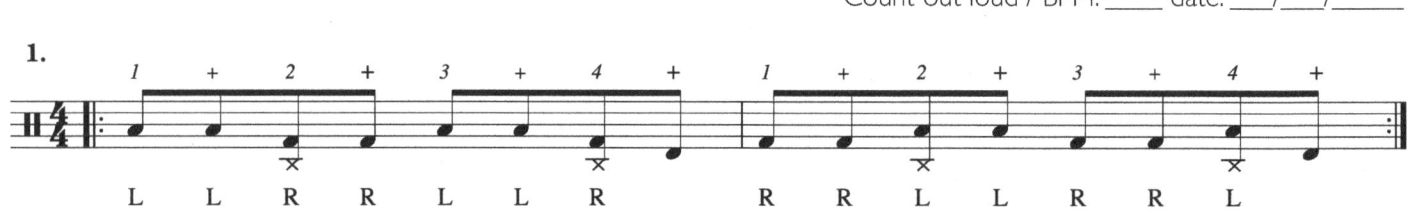

With snare drum and tom-tom:

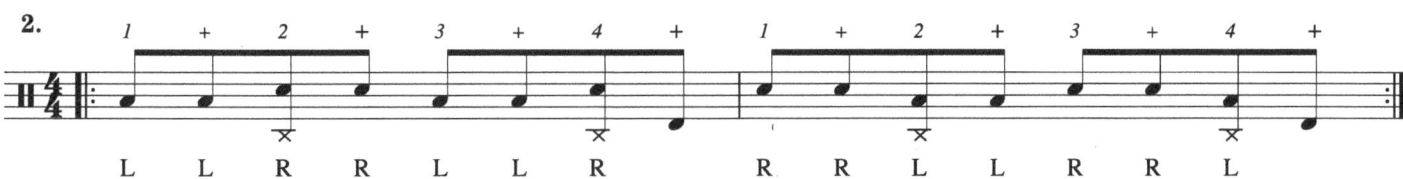

Tom-tom and floor tom:

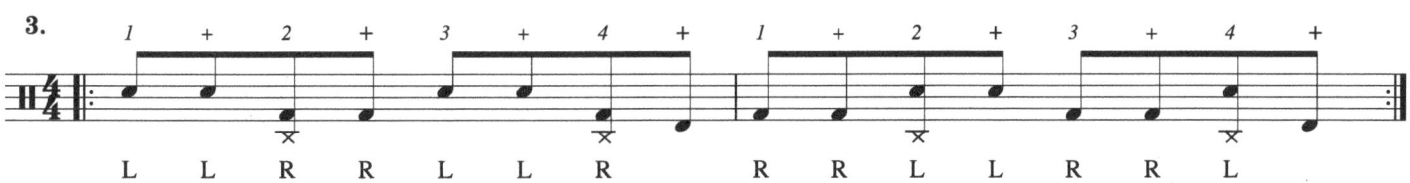

Combine:

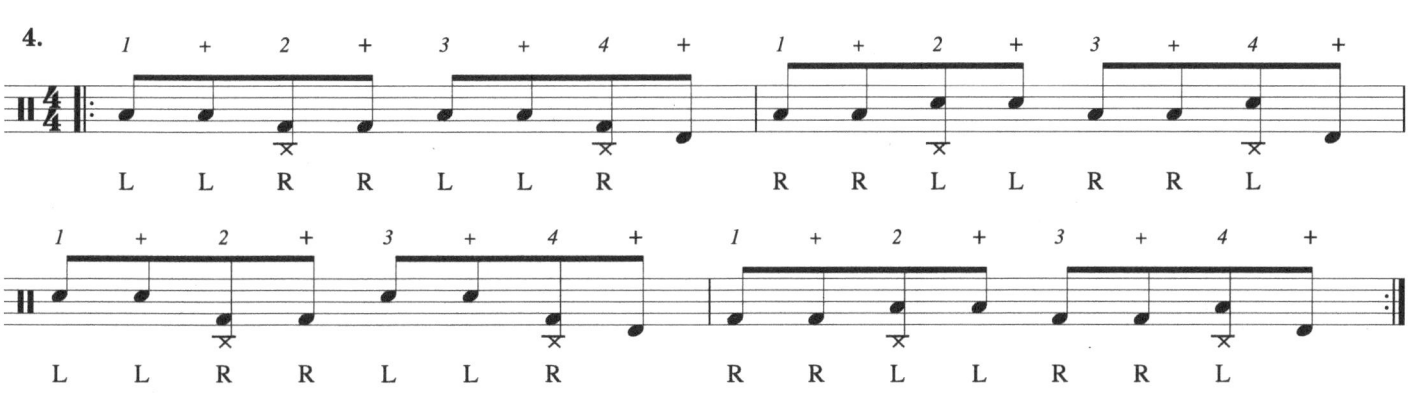

LESSON 57
The Seven-Stroke Roll

With cymbal crash on end of phrase:

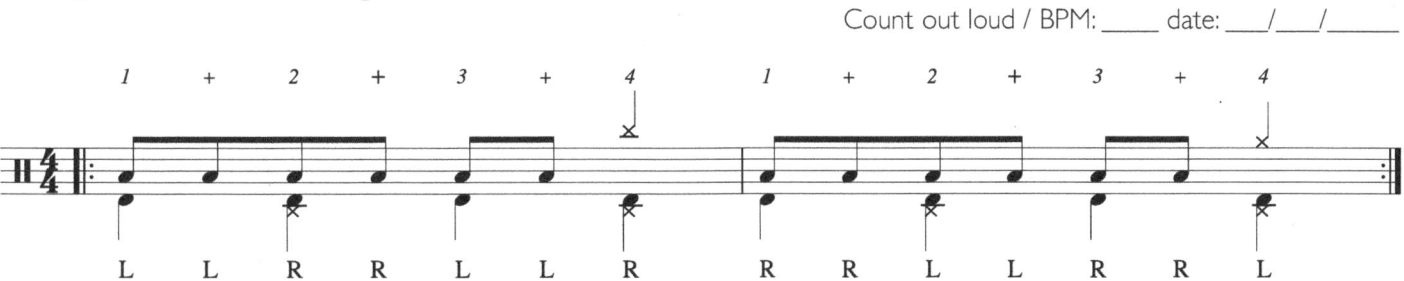

LESSON 58
Wrist Exercises for the Seven-Stroke Ruff and Roll

Alternate snare drum with bass drum:

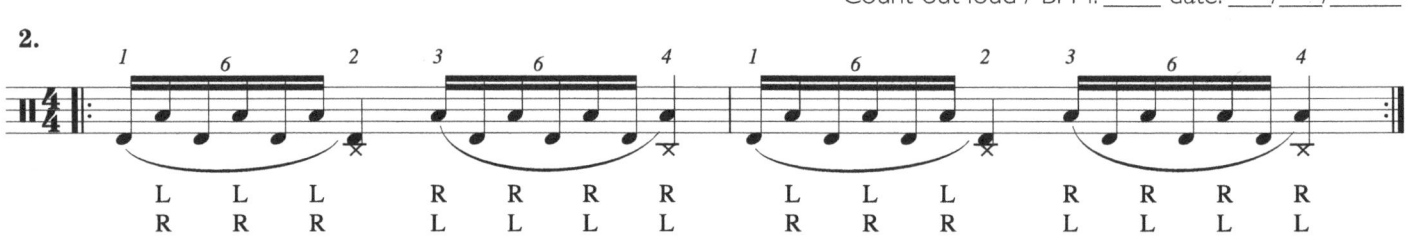

LESSON 59
The Nine-Stroke Ruff

With bass drum on every fourth stroke.

Rhythmic model:

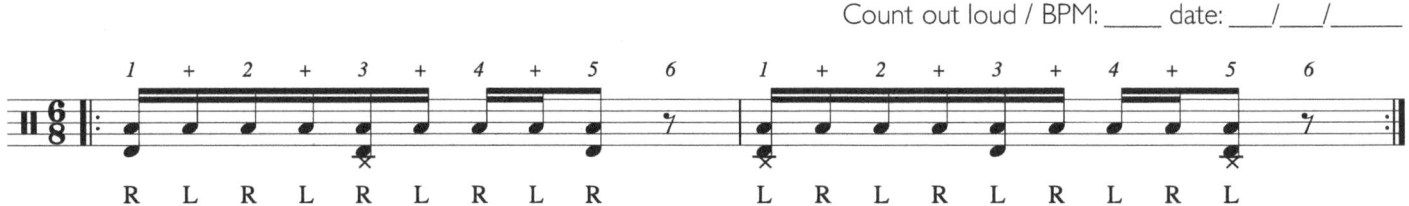

With accent on end of phrase:

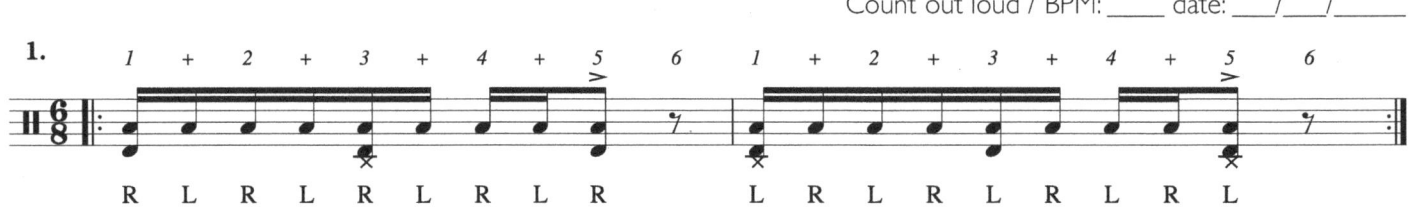

With accent on beginning of phrase:

Combine accented phrases:

LESSON 60
The Nine-Stroke Ruff

Substitute toms in place of accents.

With toms on end of phrase:

With toms on beginning of phrase:

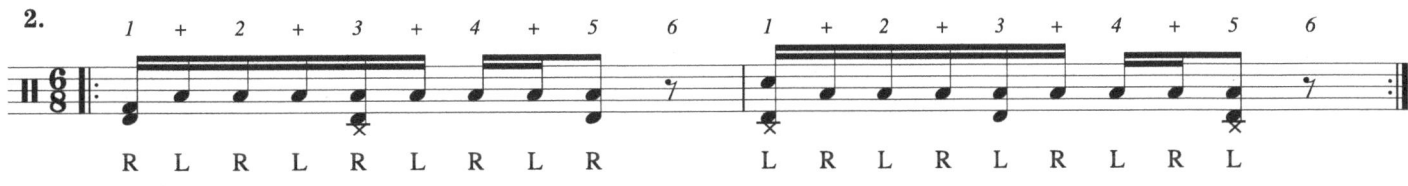

Combine 1 & 2:

Reverse, with snare drum on end of phrase:

With snare drum on beginning of phrase:

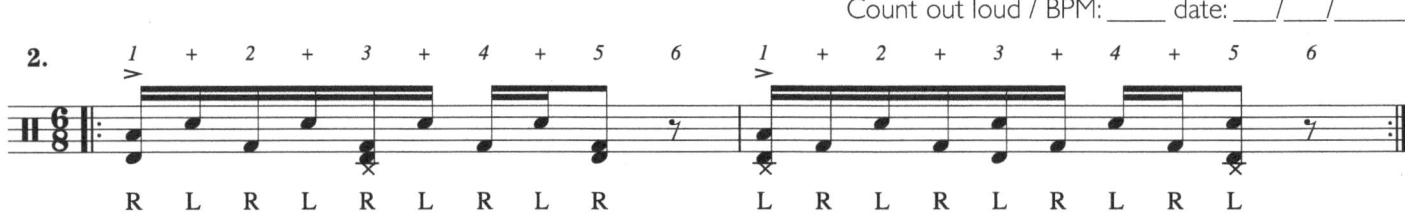

Combine 1 & 2:

LESSON 61
The Nine-Stroke Ruff

Separate hands, one hand per drum.

Floor tom and snare drum:

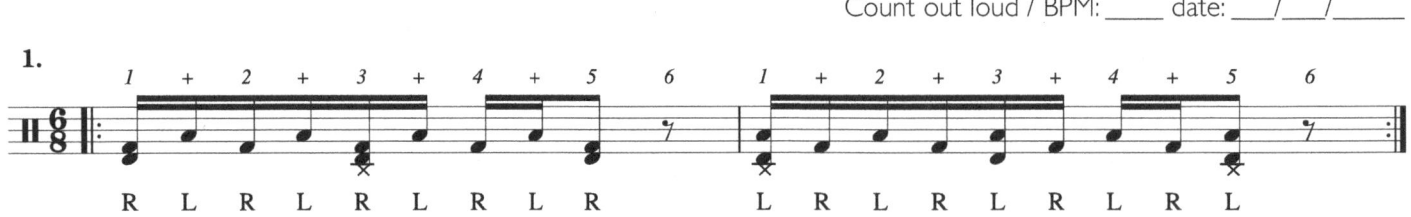

Snare drum and tom:

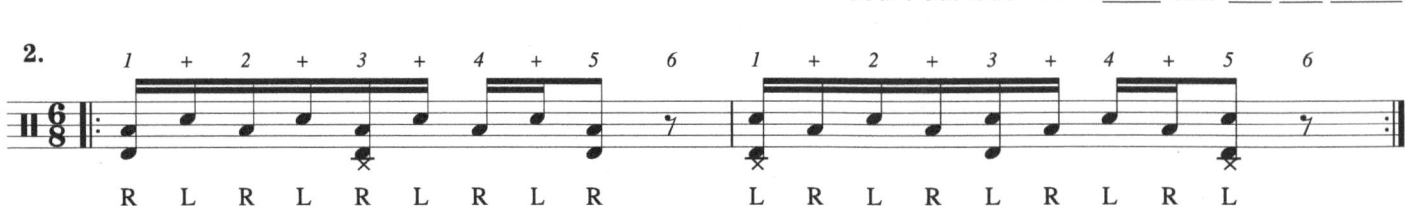

Floor tom and tom:

Combinations:

LESSON 62
The Nine-Stroke Ruff

With crash cymbals on the last beat of the phrase and on the first beat of phrase. Feather the bass drum, accenting on cymbal crashes.

With cymbals and bass drum on last beat of phrase:

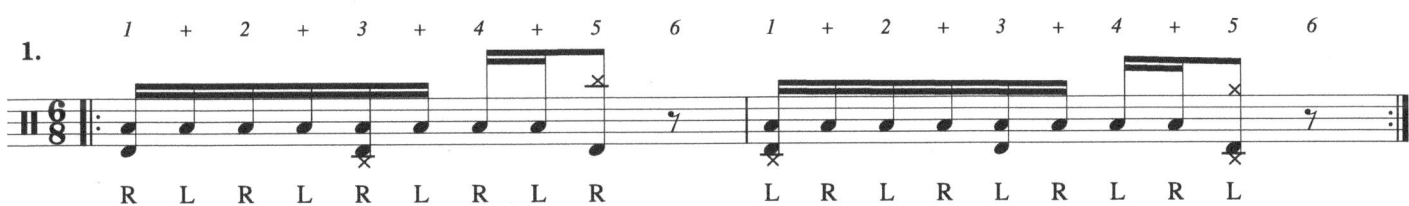

With cymbals and bass drum on first beat of phrase:

Combine both exercises:

LESSON 63
The Nine-Stroke Ruff

With the bass drum on the sixth beat. After developing the accents, deliver the accented strokes to the toms and cymbals.

Rhythmic model:

Add accents on last beat of phrase:

Accents on first beat of phrase:

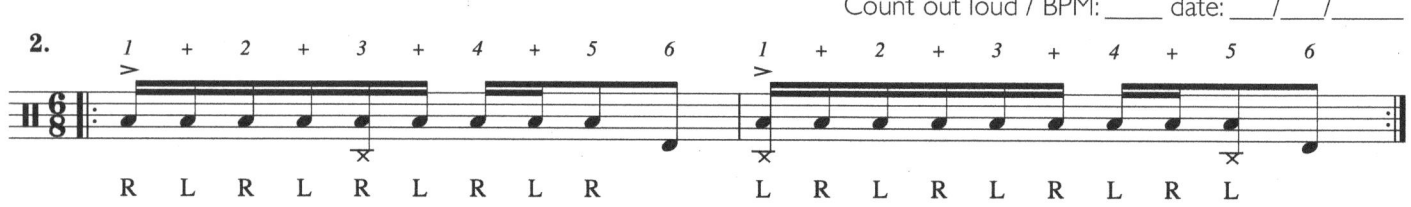

Combination of accents:

LESSON 64
The Nine-Stroke Ruff Around the Kit

Hand-to-hand exercises around the kit.

Move clockwise around the kit:

Move counterclockwise around the kit:

LESSON 65
The Nine-Stroke Roll

With bass drum on every fourth stroke.

Rhythmic model:

With accents on last beat of phrase:

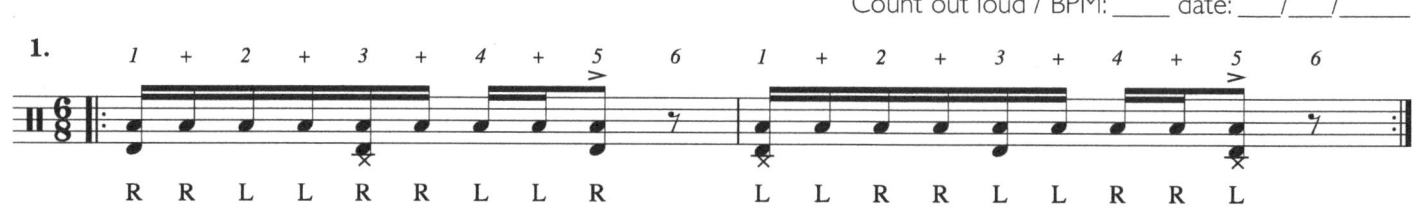

Accents on first beat of phrase:

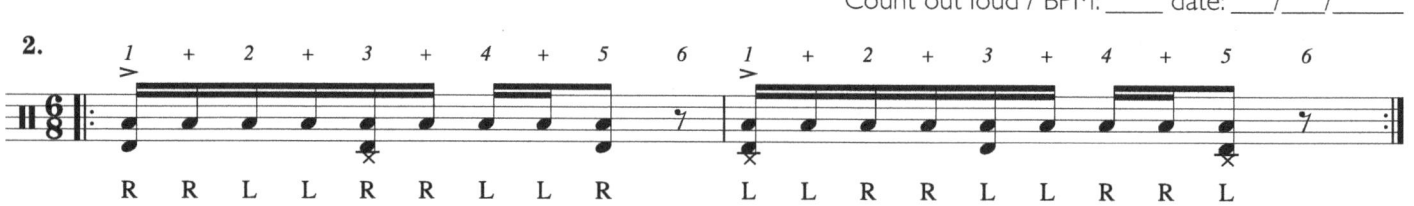

Combine 1 & 2:

LESSON 66
The Nine-Stroke Roll

Substitute toms in place of accents.

With toms in place of accents:

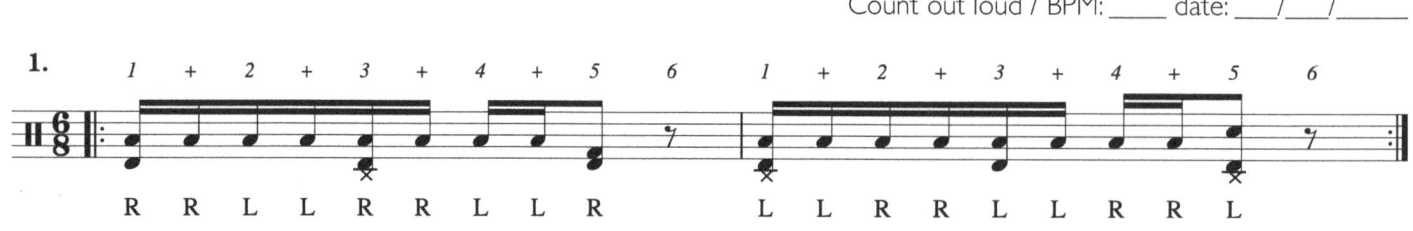

Reverse, with snare receiving accents:

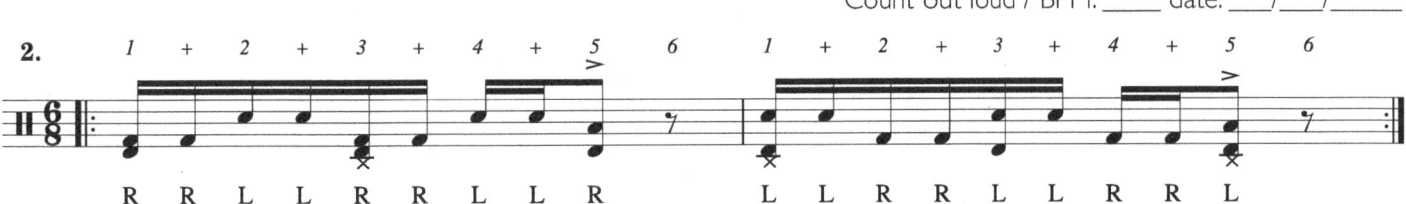

Combine 1 & 2:

LESSON 67
The Nine-Stroke Roll

Separate hands, one hand per drum.

Floor tom and snare drum:

Snare drum and tom:

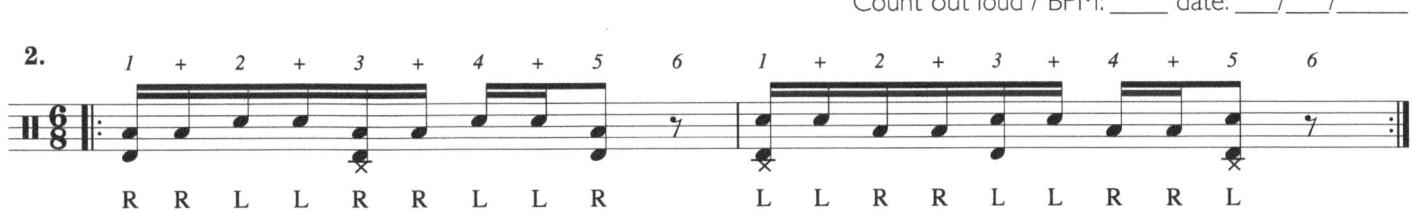

Floor tom and tom-tom:

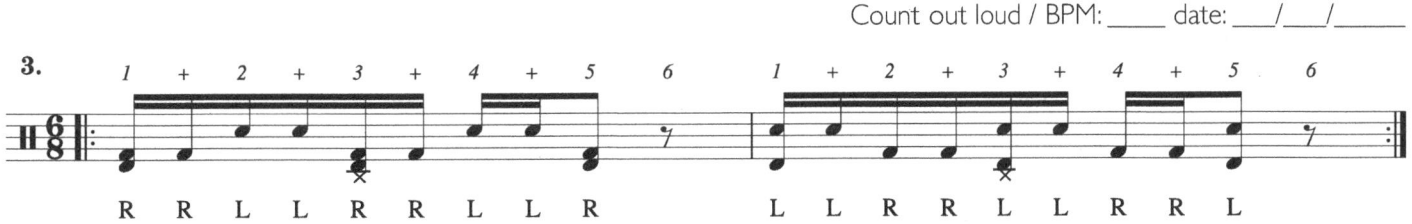

Combinations:

LESSON 68
The Nine-Stroke Roll

Crash cymbals at the end of the phrase. Feather the bass drum, accenting on cymbal crashes.

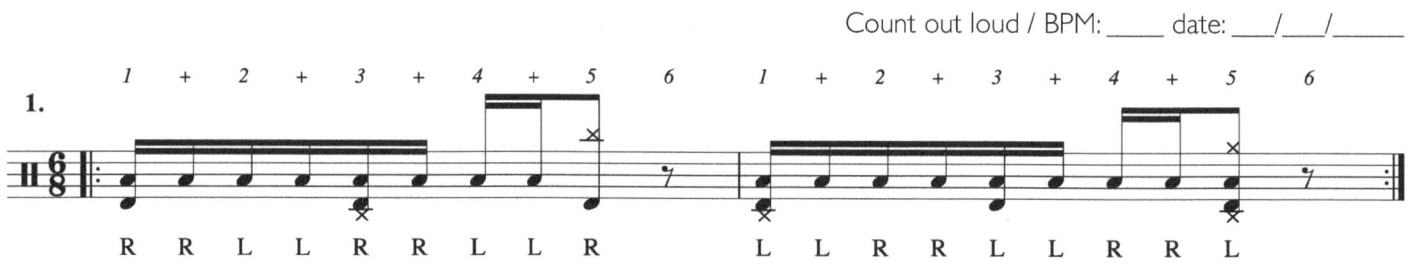

LESSON 69
The Nine-Stroke Roll

With bass drum on the sixth beat.

Rhythmic model:

Accent on last beat of phrase:

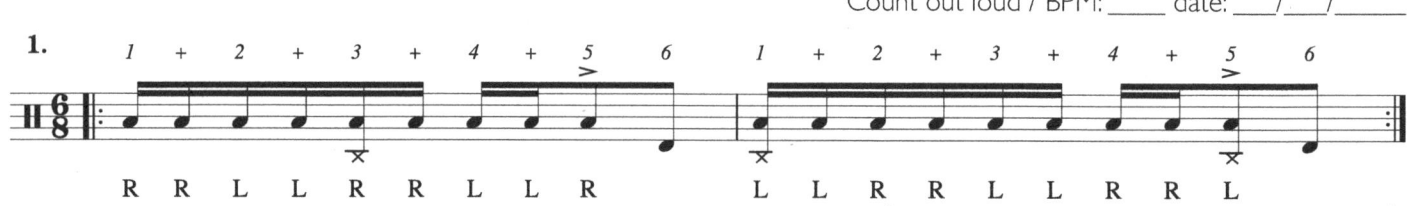

Accent on first beat of phrase:

Combine accented phrases:

LESSON 70
The Nine-Stroke Roll

With bass drum on sixth beat. Substitute accents with toms.

With toms on end of phrase:

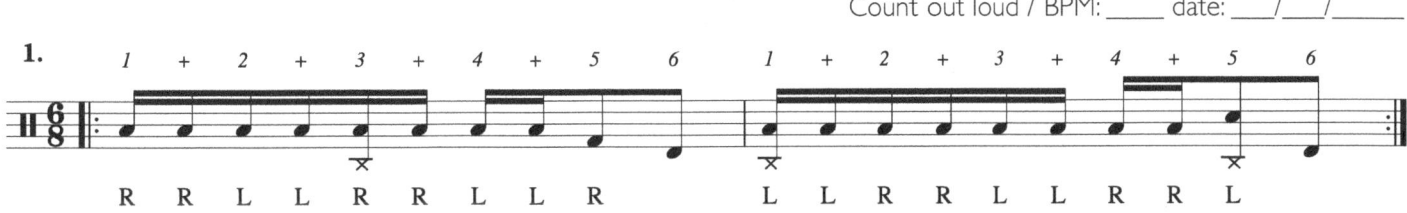

Reverse, with snare drum on end of phrase:

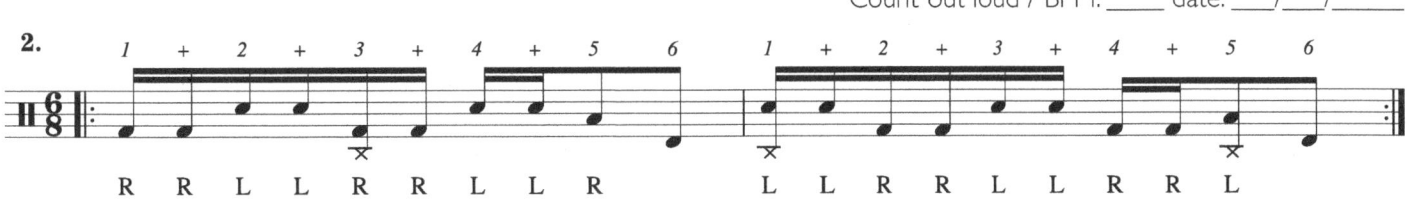

Combine 1 & 2:

LESSON 71
The Nine-Stroke Roll

Bass drum on sixth beat, separate hands.

Separate hands, floor tom and snare drum:

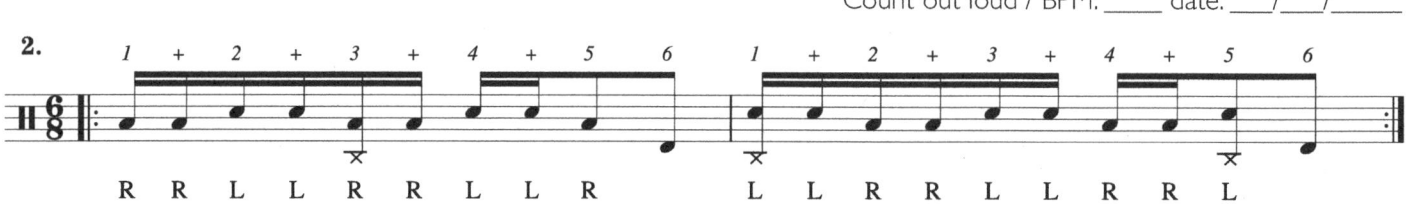

Separate hands, snare drum and tom-tom:

Separate hands, tom-tom and floor tom:

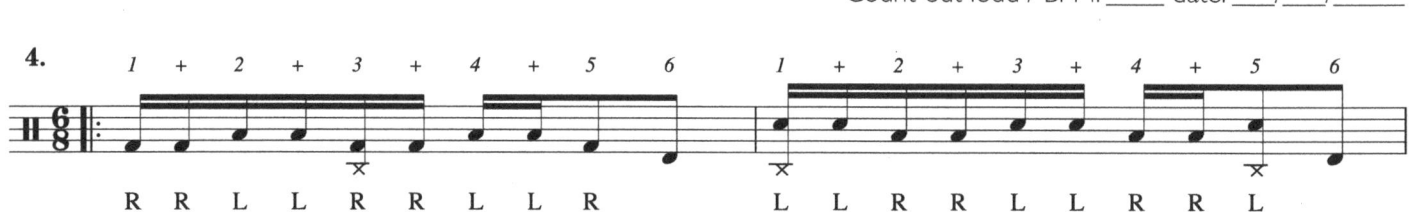

Combine:

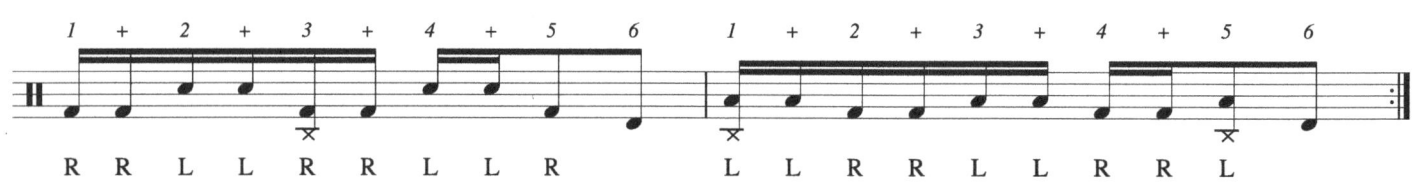

LESSON 72
The Nine-Stroke Roll Around the Kit

Snare drum, tom-tom and floor tom; move clockwise around the kit:

Move counterclockwise around the kit:

Floor tom, snare drum and tom:

LESSON 73
Wrist Exercise for the Nine-Stroke Ruff and Roll

1.

Exchange alternating single strokes with bass drum and snare drum:

2.

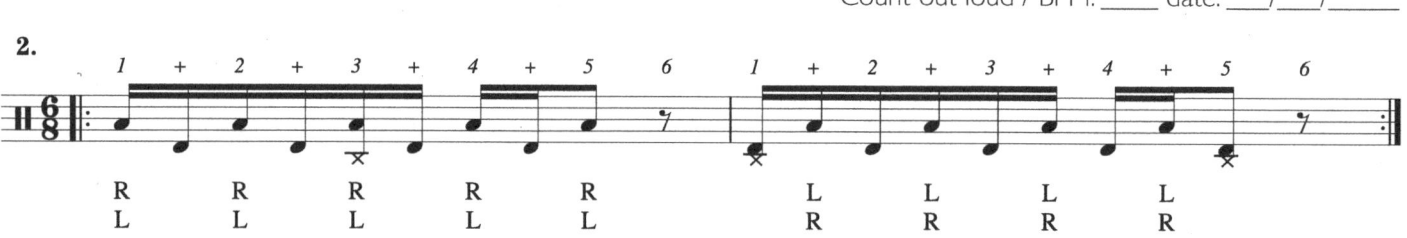

It is imperative for the kit drummer to master the double-stroke roll, with the second double-stroke on each hand being an accented stroke. *The Ultimate Drummer's Workout* is an excellent method for perfecting the double-stroke roll.

LESSON 74
The Double-Stroke Roll Around the Kit ▶

With the downbeat on the right hand.

Rhythmic model:

Clockwise around the kit:

1.

72

Counterclockwise around the kit:

Combine 1 & 2:

LESSON 75
The Double-Stroke Roll Around the Kit

With the downbeat on the left hand.

Rhythmic model:

Clockwise around the kit:

Counterclockwise around the kit:

Combine 1 & 2:

LESSON 76
The Double-Stroke Roll Around the Kit

Triplet rhythm; bass drum on every sixth stroke.

Rhythmic model:

Clockwise around the kit:

Counterclockwise around the kit:

Count out loud / BPM: _____ date: ___/___/_____

L L R R L L R R L L R R   L L R R L L R R L L R R

L L R R L L R R L L R R   L L R R L L R R L L R R

Combine 1 & 2:

Count out loud / BPM: _____ date: ___/___/_____

L L R R L L R R L L R R   L L R R L L R R L L R R

L L R R L L R R L L R R   L L R R L L R R L L R R

L L R R L L R R L L R R   L L R R L L R R L L R R

LESSON 77
The Press Roll

With downbeat on the right hand:

With downbeat on the left hand:

With downbeat on every third pulse:

LESSON 78
The Single Paradiddle

With the downbeat on every other stroke.

Rhythmic model:

Substitute accent with initial strokes on tom-tom:

Accents on tom-tom and floor tom:

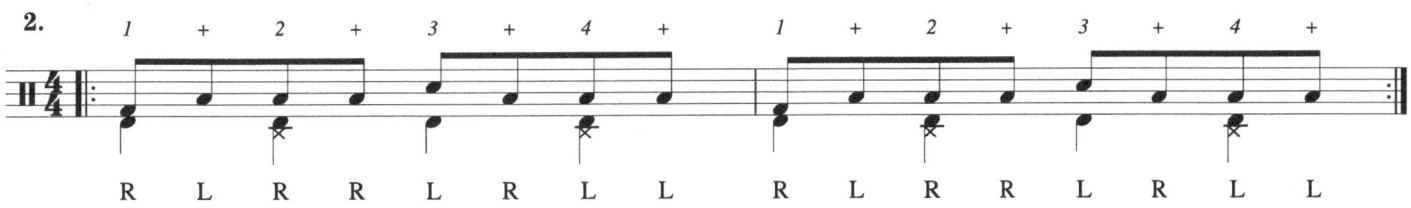

Combine 1 & 2:

Reverse from tom-toms, with initial strokes on snare drum:

Reverse with initial strokes on tom and floor tom:

Combine 1 & 2:

LESSON 79
The Single Paradiddle Around the Kit

Moving clockwise:

Moving counterclockwise:

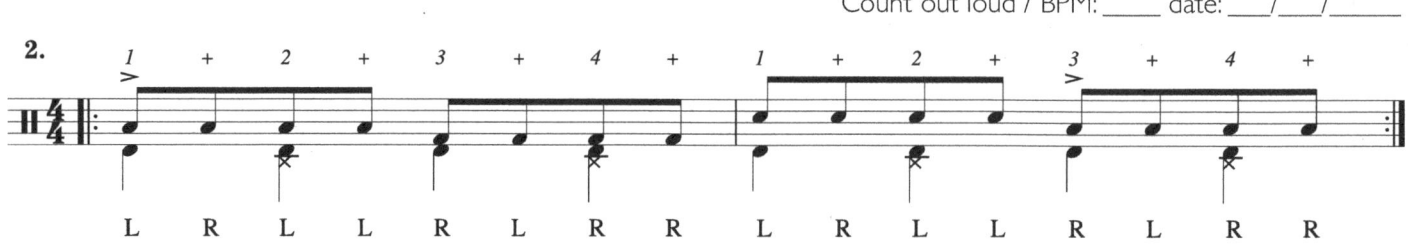

LESSON 80
The Single Paradiddle

With accents on the crash cymbals. Feather the bass drum, accenting on cymbal crashes.

Crashes on the initial strokes:

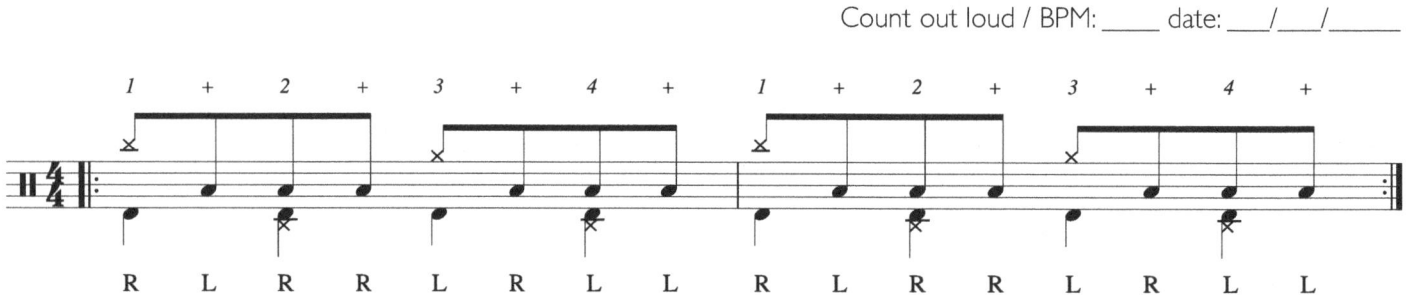

LESSON 81
The Single Paradiddle

Except for the added accent, this is the same as the previous rudiment.

Rhythmic model:

Count out loud / BPM: ____ date: ___/___/___

Apply accents to tom-tom:

Count out loud / BPM: ____ date: ___/___/___

Accents on floor tom and tom-tom:

Count out loud / BPM: ____ date: ___/___/___

Combine 1 & 2:

Count out loud / BPM: ____ date: ___/___/___

Reverse accents from tom to snare drum:

Reverse accents from tom-tom and floor tom to snare drum:

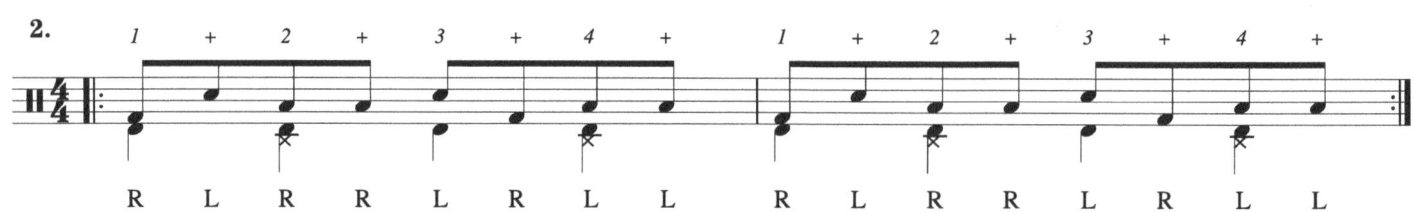

Combine 1 & 2:

LESSON 82
The Single Paradiddle

With accents on the crash cymbals:

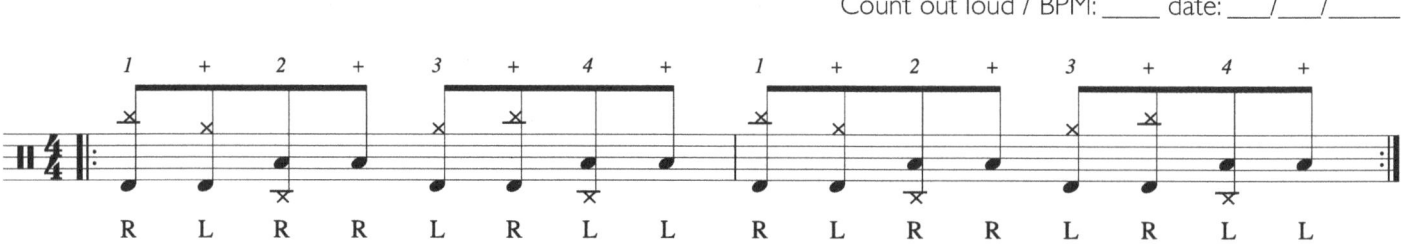

LESSON 83
The Single Paradiddle

Snare drum and bass drum:

Count out loud / BPM: _____ date: ___/___/_____

1.

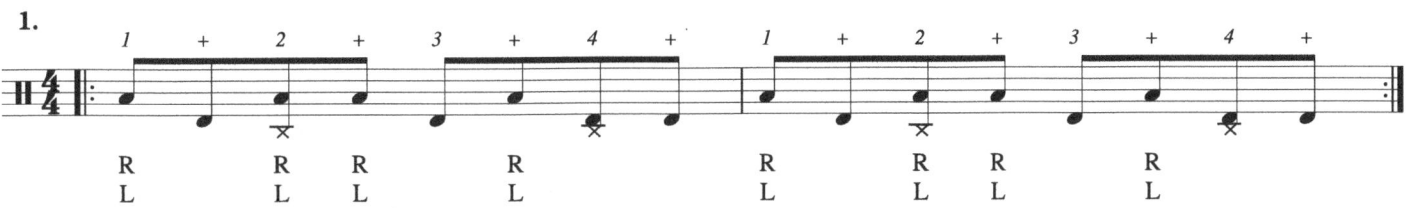

Reverse:

Count out loud / BPM: _____ date: ___/___/_____

2.

LESSON 84
The Double Paradiddle (A)

With bass drum on every other beat, subdivide with the hi-hat.

Rhythmic model:

Count out loud / BPM: _____ date: ___/___/_____

Develop accents to tom-tom:

Count out loud / BPM: _____ date: ___/___/_____

1.

Accents on floor tom and tom-tom:

Count out loud / BPM: _____ date: ___/___/_____

2.

Combine 1 & 2:

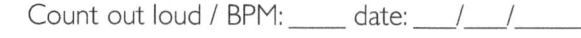

Reverse accents from snare drum to tom-tom:

Reverse accents from tom-toms to snare drum:

Combine 1 & 2:

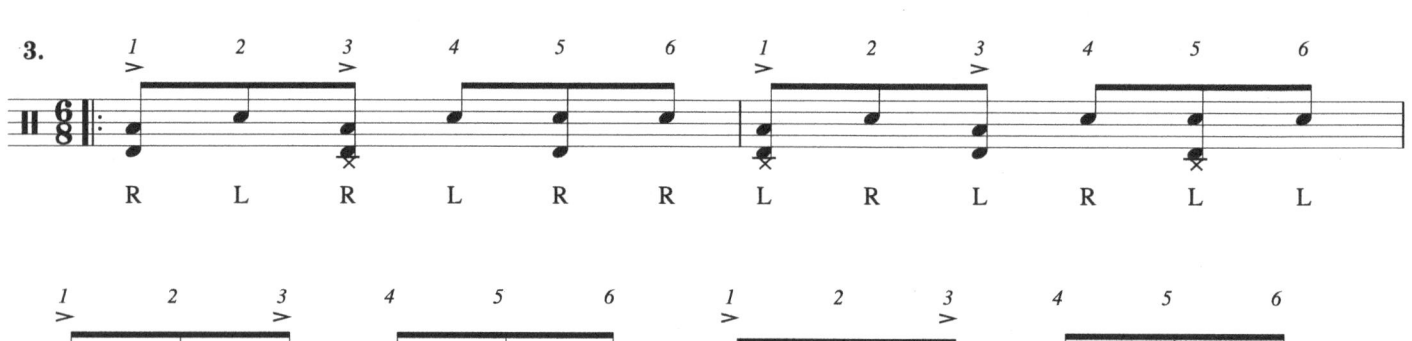

LESSON 85
The Double Paradiddle (A)

With cymbal crashes on *1* and *2*. Feather the bass drum, accenting on cymbal crashes.

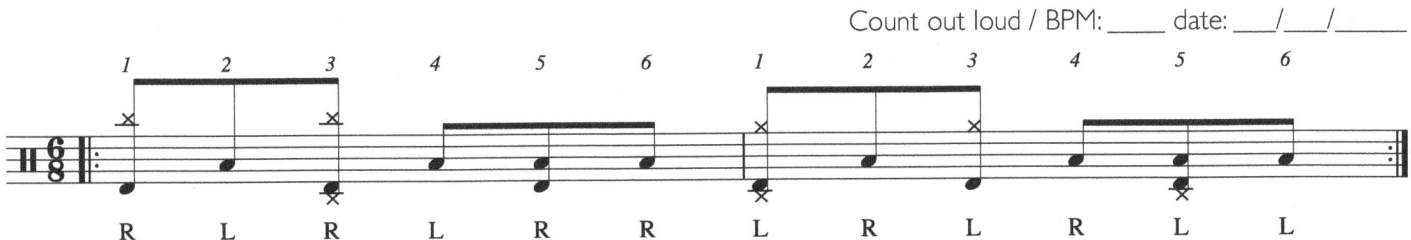

LESSON 86
The Double Paradiddle (B)

With one accent; foot on *1*, *2* and *3*.

Rhythmic model:

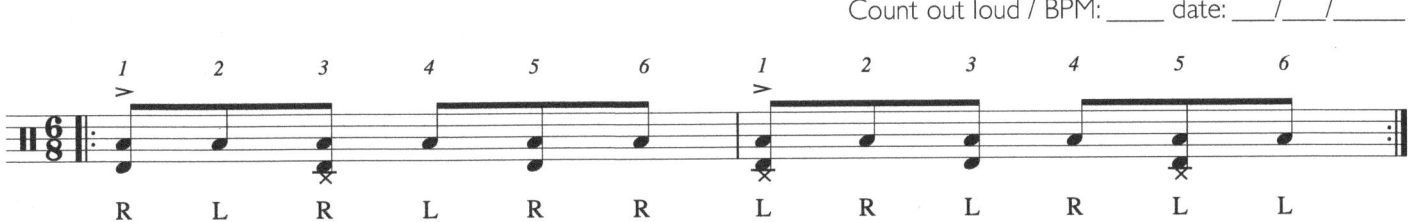

Substitute accent with tom-tom:

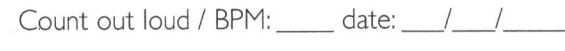

1.

Substitute accents with tom-tom and floor tom:

2.

Combine 1 & 2:

3.

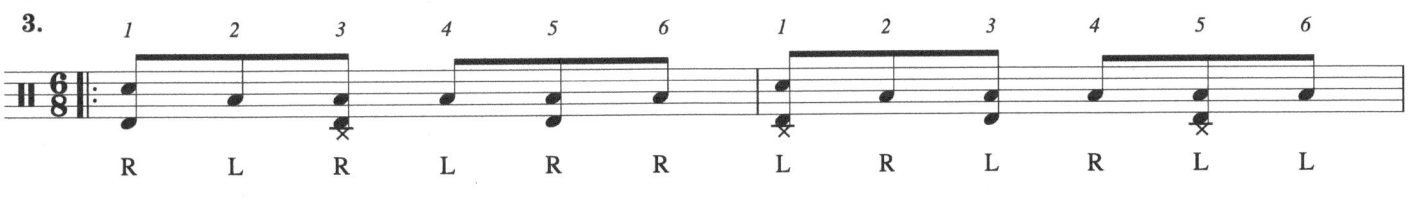

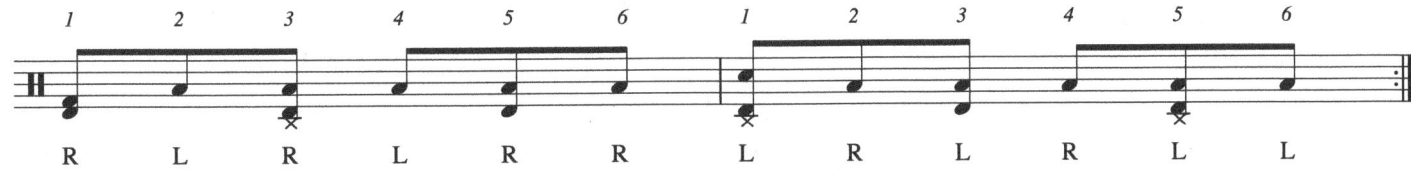

83

Reverse from tom-tom, accented strokes on snare drum:

Reverse from tom-tom and floor tom, with accented strokes on snare drum:

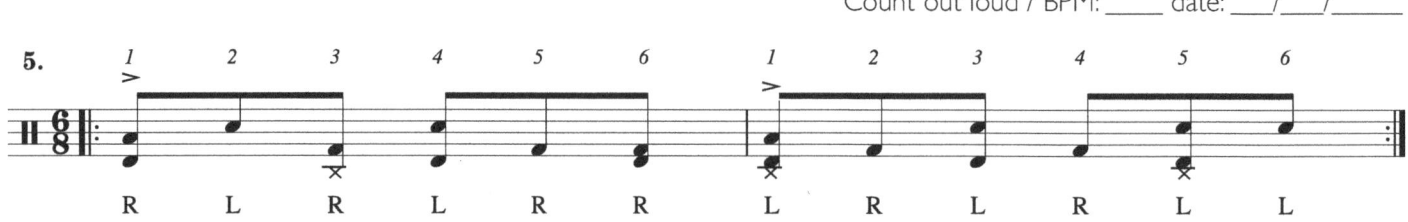

Combine 4 & 5:

LESSON 87
The Double Paradiddle Around the Kit

Moving clockwise:

Moving counterclockwise:

LESSON 88
The Double Paradiddle (A)

With cymbal crashes on the initial stroke. Feather the bass drum, accenting with the cymbal crashes.

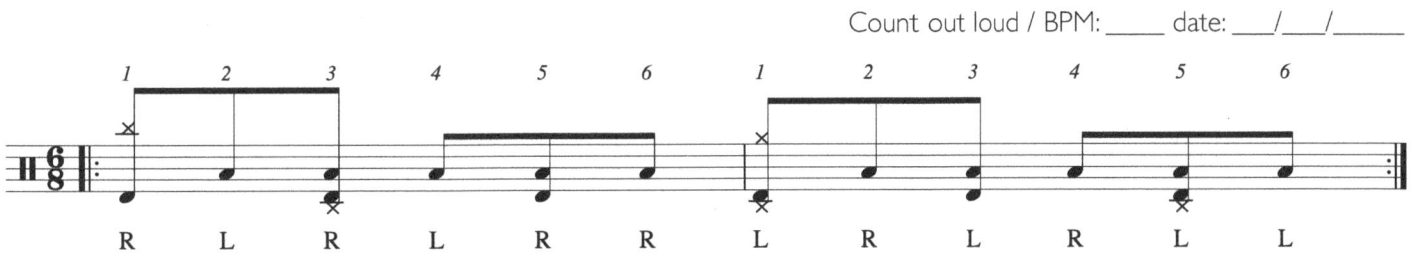

LESSON 89
The Double Paradiddle (B)

Snare drum and bass drum:

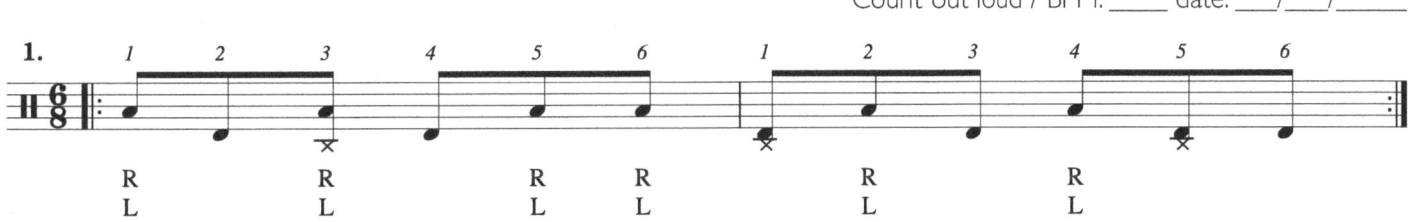

Reverse:

LESSON 90
The Triple Paradiddle

With bass drum downbeat on every other stroke.

Rhythmic model:

Accent on the first, third and fifth strokes:

1.

Place accented strokes on tom-tom:

2.

Accented strokes on tom-tom and floor tom:

3.

Combine 1 & 2:

4.

Reverse accents on snare from tom-tom:

Reverse accents to snare from tom-toms:

Combine 1 & 2:

LESSON 91
The Triple Paradiddle

With crash cymbals on accents:

LESSON 92
The Triple Paradiddle

With accents on the first, third and sixth strokes.

Rhythmic model:

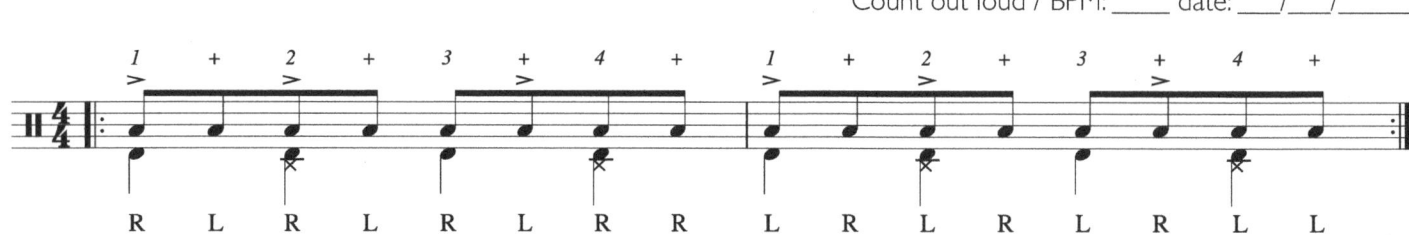

Place accents on tom-tom:

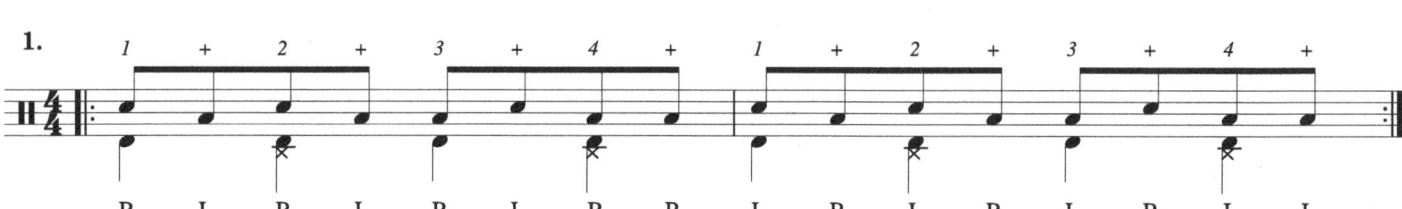

Place accents on floor tom and tom:

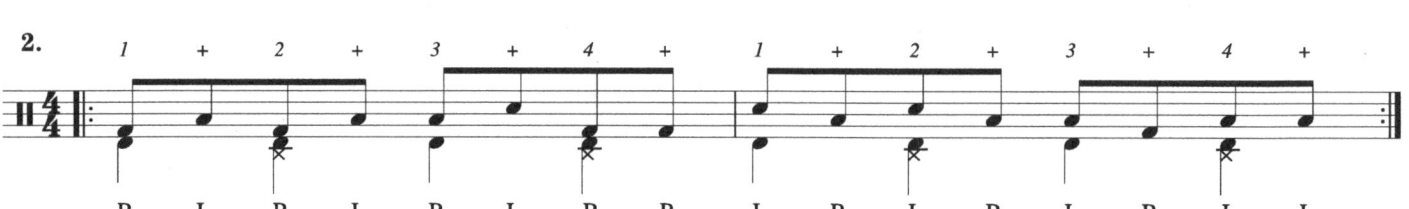

Accents on the sixth stroke to tom-toms:

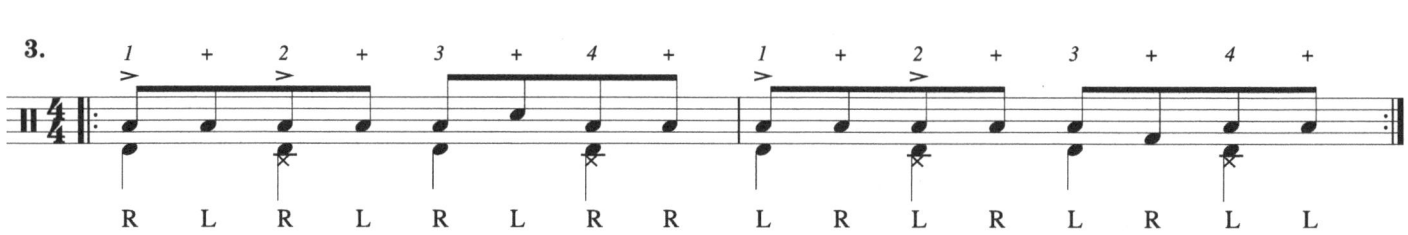

Combine 1, 2 & 3:

Reverse accents to snare drum:

Reverse accent on sixth stroke to snare drum:

Combine 1 & 2:

LESSON 93
The Triple Paradiddle Around the Kit

Clockwise around the kit:

Counterclockwise around the kit:

LESSON 94
The Triple Paradiddle

With crash cymbals and bass drum on accented strokes.

First and third strokes on crash cymbals:

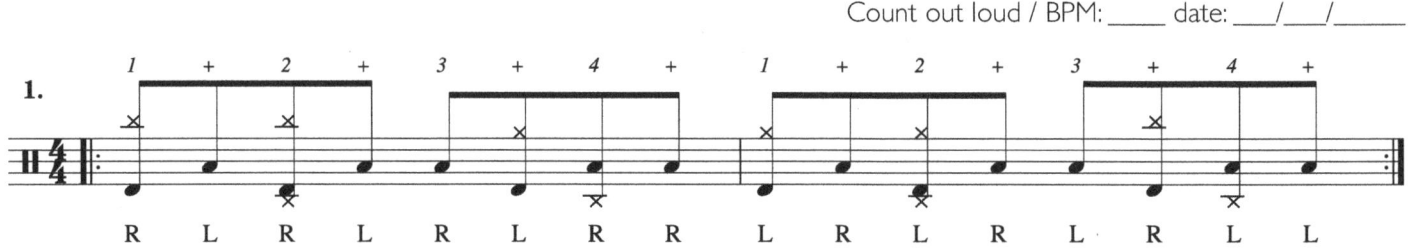

With sixth stroke on crashes:

Combine 1 & 2:

90

LESSON 95
The Triple Paradiddle

Bass drum and snare drum:

Count out loud / BPM: _____ date: ___/___/_____

1.

```
R   R   R   R R       L   L   L
 L   L   L   L  L   R   R   R   R
```

Reverse:

Count out loud / BPM: _____ date: ___/___/_____

2.
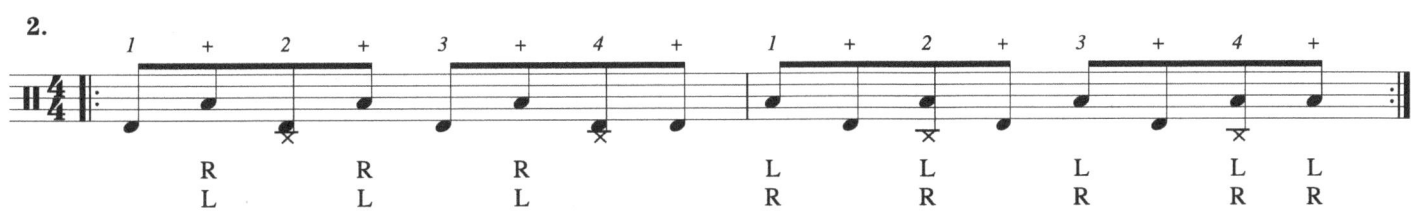

```
R   R   R       L   L   L   L   L
 L   L   L       R   R   R   R   R
```

LESSON 96
The Flam Around the Kit

With bass drum on the accented alternated strokes.

Rhythmic model:

Count out loud / BPM: _____ date: ___/___/_____

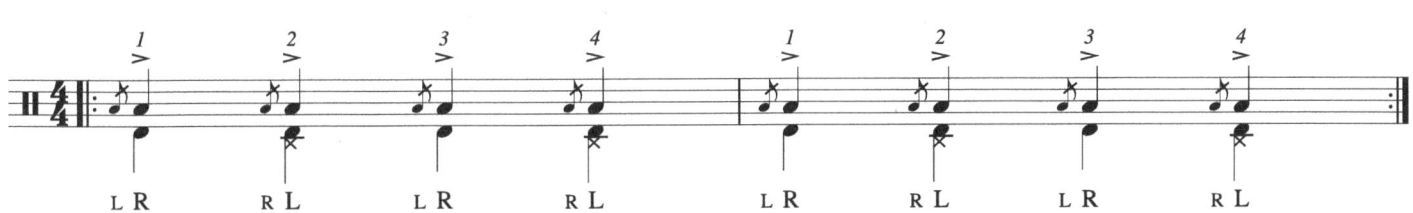

```
L R   R L   L R   R L     L R   R L   L R   R L
```

Clockwise around the kit:

Count out loud / BPM: _____ date: ___/___/_____

1.
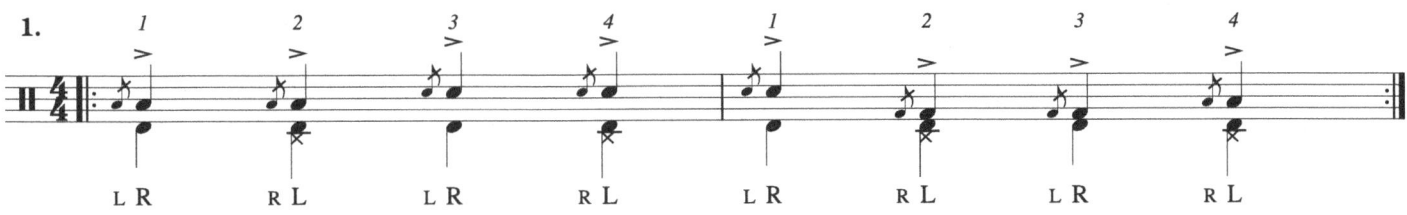

```
L R   R L   L R   R L     L R   R L   L R   R L
```

Counterclockwise around the kit:

Count out loud / BPM: _____ date: ___/___/_____

2.
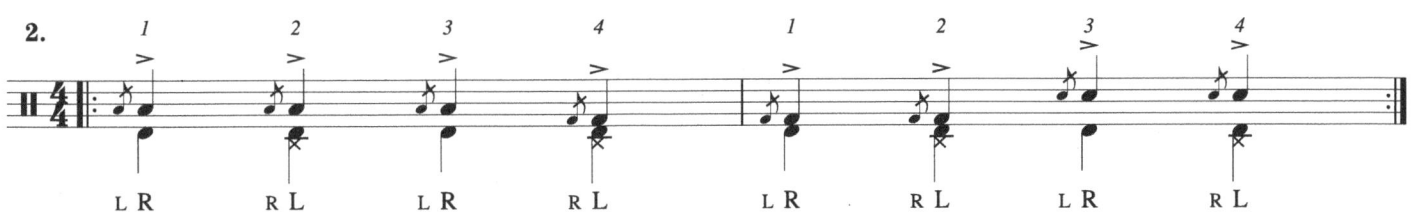

```
L R   R L   L R   R L     L R   R L   L R   R L
```

Flams with grace notes remaining on the snare drum:

LESSON 97
The Flam

Right-hand flams and left-hand flams.

Rhythmic model:

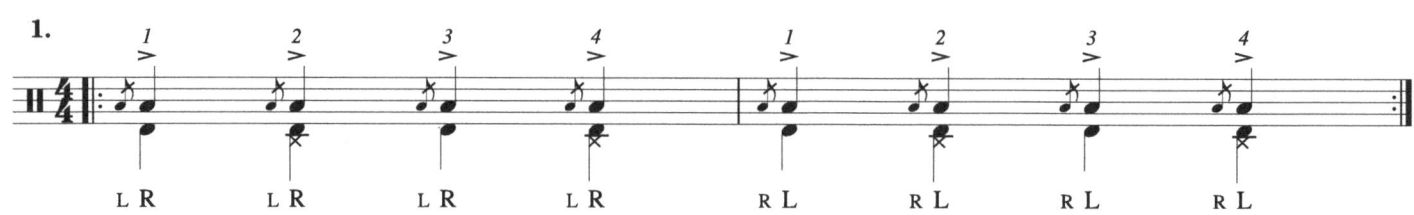

Combine right-hand and left-hand flams:

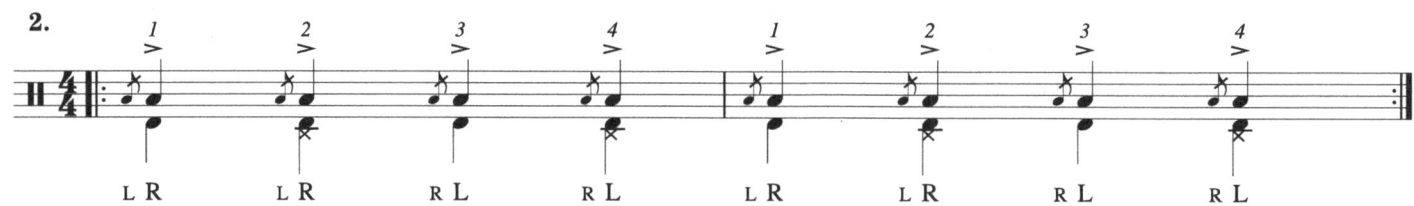

Combine 1 & 2:

LESSON 98
The Flam

With bass drum on the *and*s:

1.

Share initial stroke with floor tom and tom:

2.

Combine 1 & 2:

3.

LESSON 99
The Single Flam Paradiddle (Flamadiddle)

Rhythmic model:

With initial strokes on tom-tom:

1.
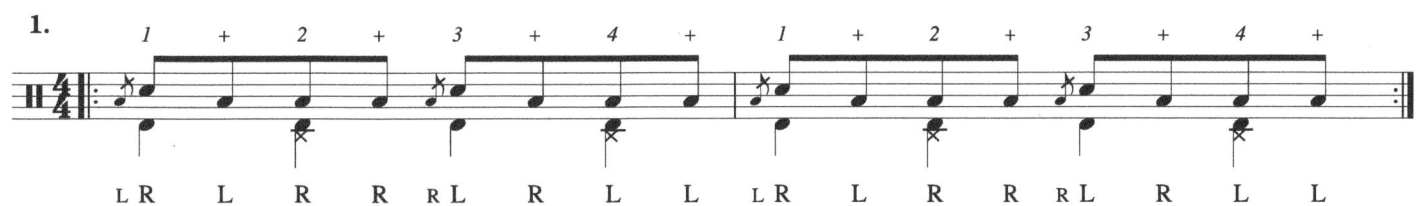

With initial stroke on floor tom:

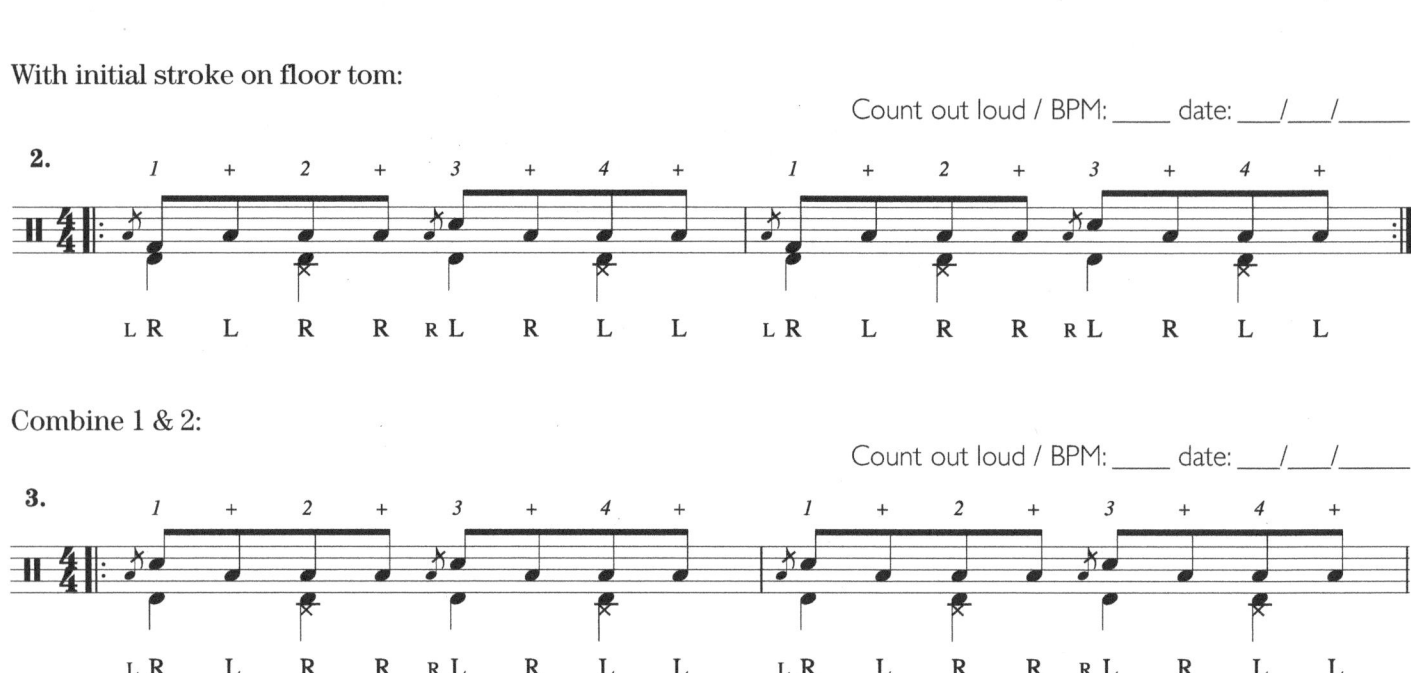

Combine 1 & 2:

Reverse, with initial strokes on snare drum from tom-tom:

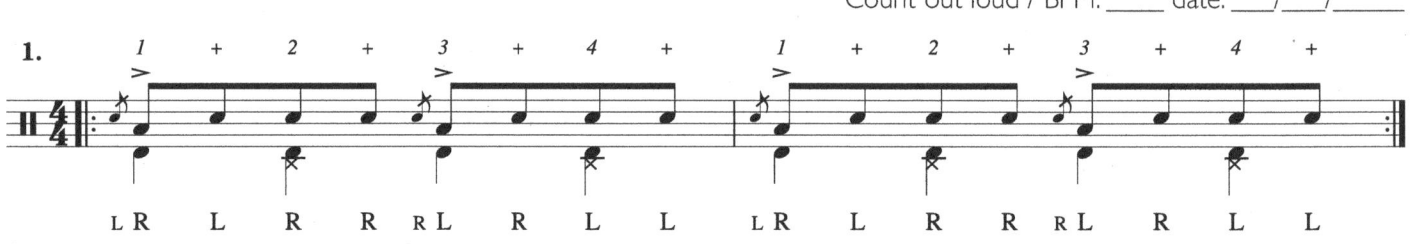

Reverse, with initial strokes from tom-tom and floor tom:

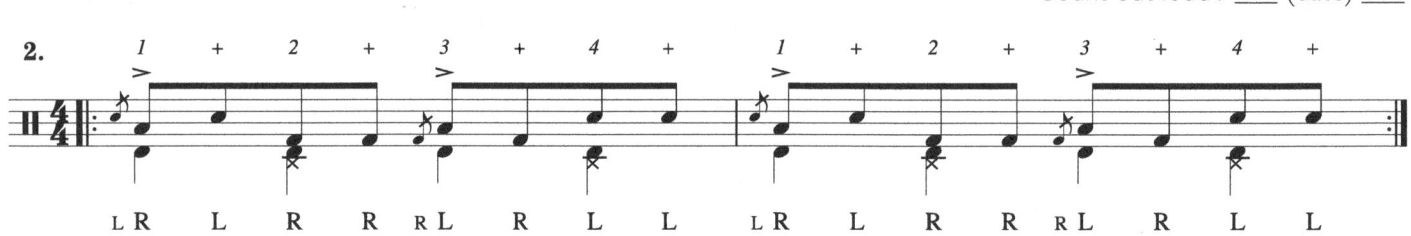

Combine 1 & 2:

LESSON 100
The Double Flam Paradiddle (Flama-Flamadiddle)

Rhythmic model:

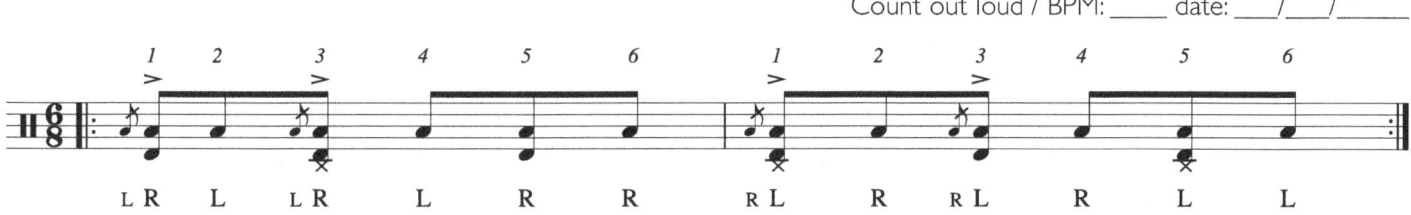

With initial strokes on tom-tom:

With initial strokes on tom-toms:

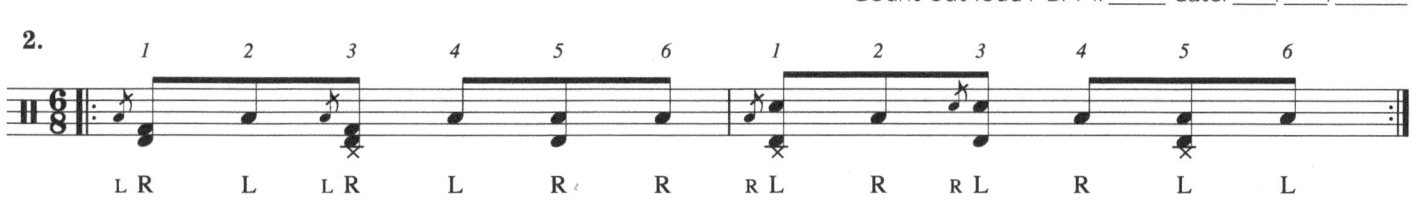

Combine 1 & 2:

Reverse, with initial strokes on snare drum from tom-tom:

Reverse, with initial strokes on snare drum from tom-tom and floor tom:

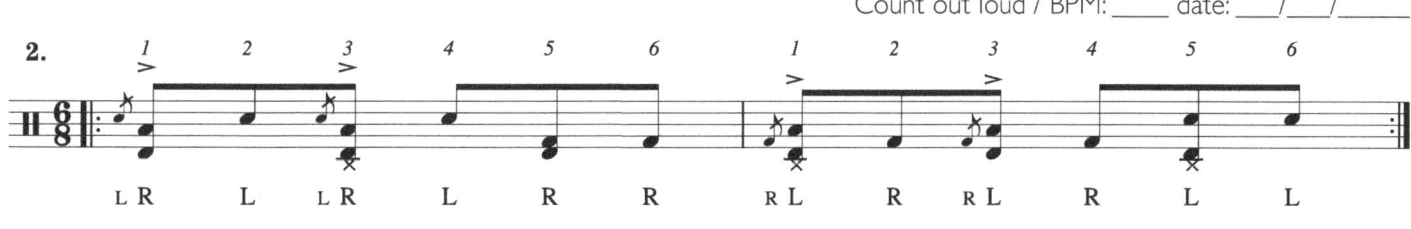

Combine 1 & 2:

LESSON 101
The Triple Flam Paradiddle (Flama-Flama-Flamadiddle)

Rhythmic model:

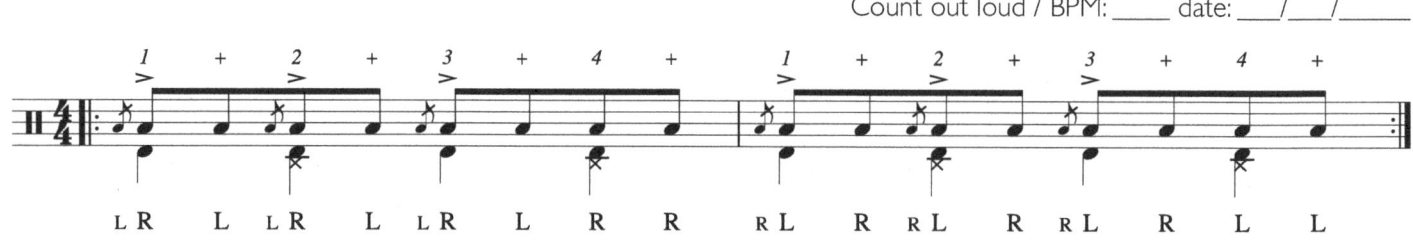

With initial strokes on tom-tom:

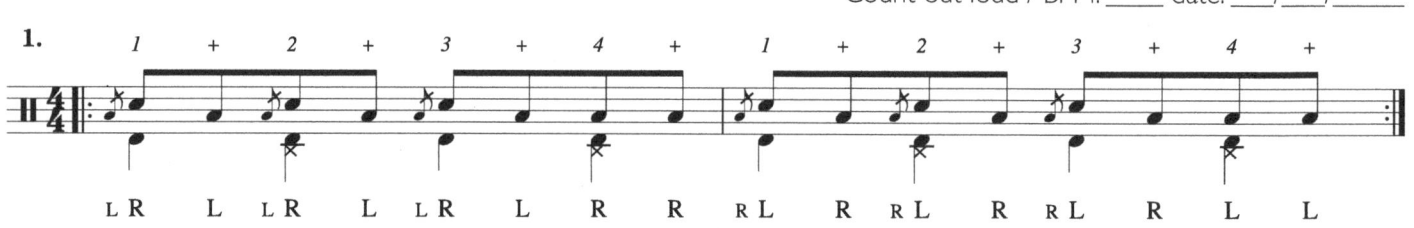

With initial strokes on floor tom and tom-tom:

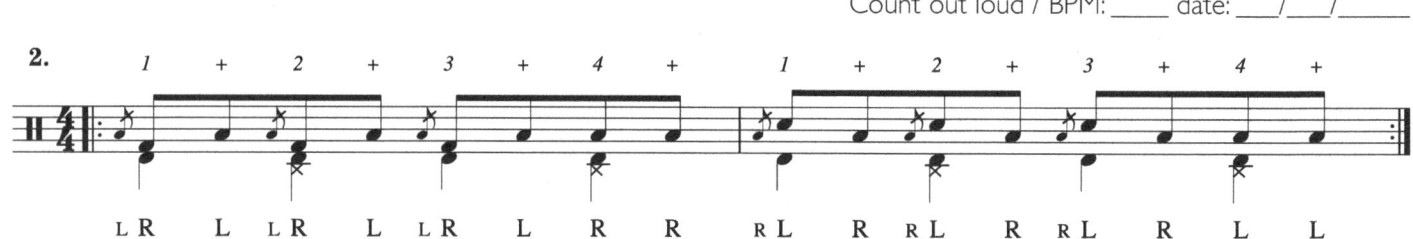

Combine 1 & 2:

3.

Reverse, with initial strokes on snare drum from tom-tom:

1.

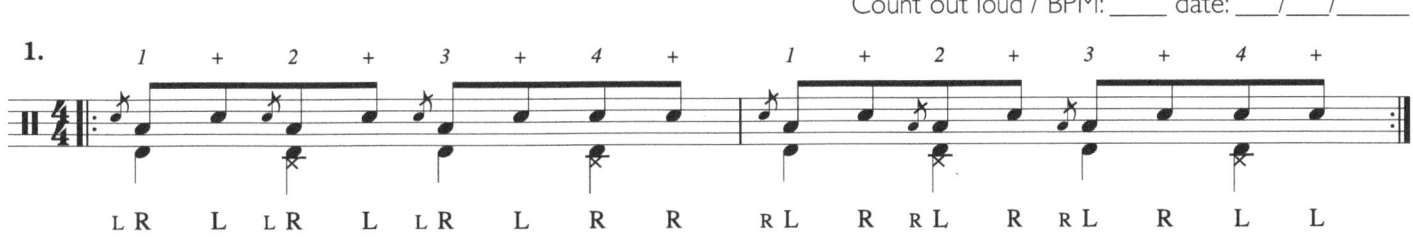

Reverse, with snare drum on initial strokes from tom-tom and floor tom:

2.

LESSON 102
The 2/4 Flam Tap

Rhythmic model:

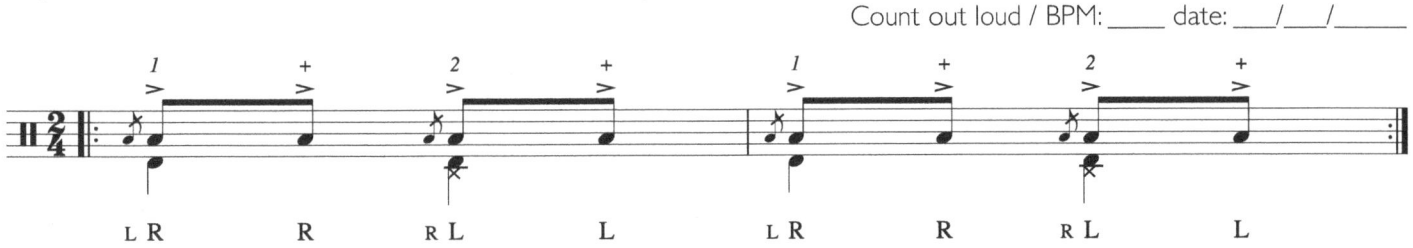

With *1* and *2* on tom:

1.

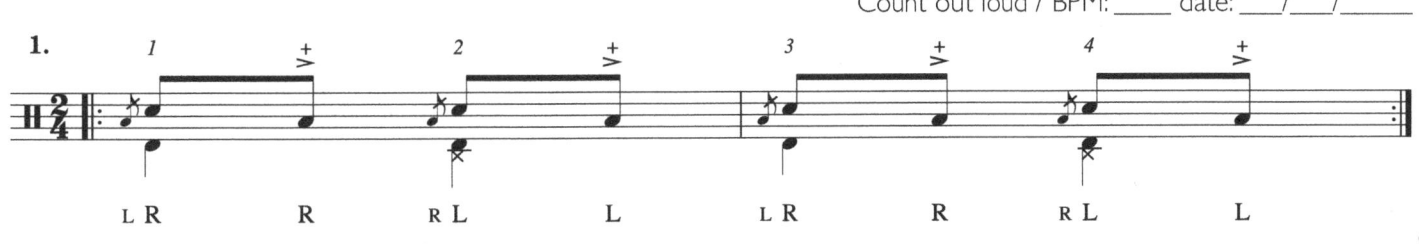

With *1* and *2* on floor tom and tom:

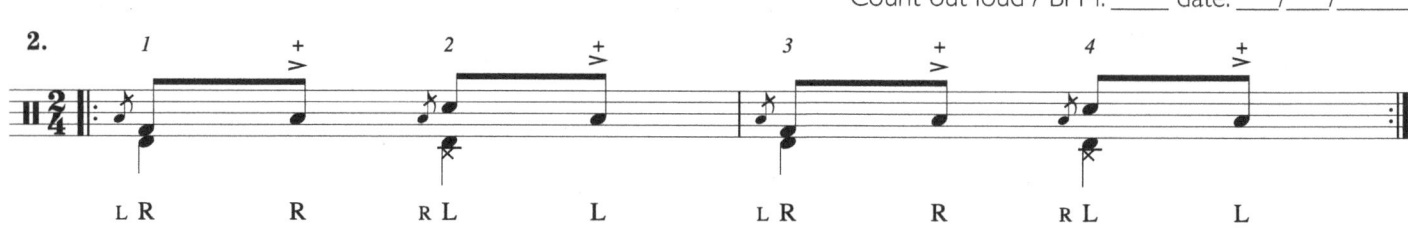

Combine 1 & 2:

With initial stroke on crash cymbals:

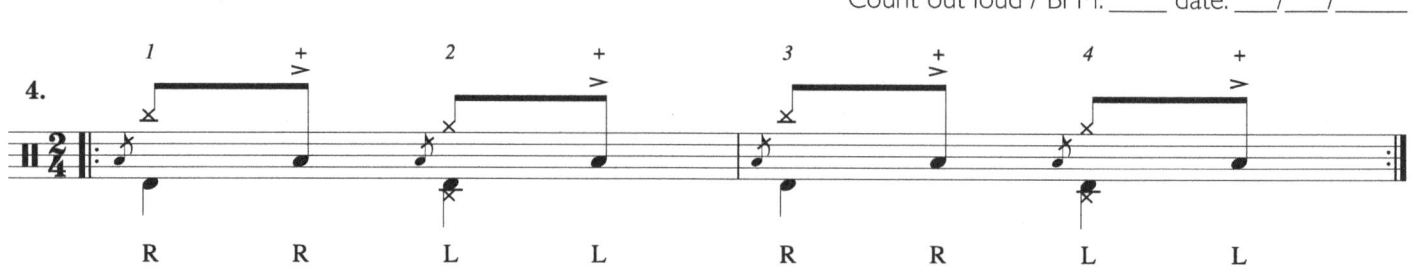

LESSON 103
The 6/8 Flam Tap

Rhythmic model:

With *1* and *4* on tom:

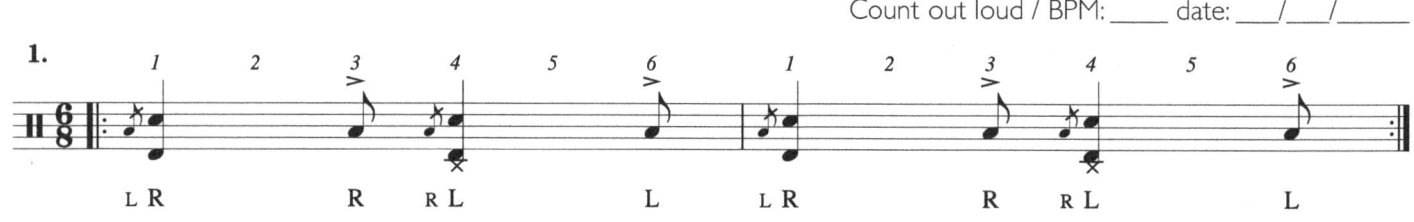

With *1* and *4* on floor tom and tom:

With crash cymbals on *1* and *4:*

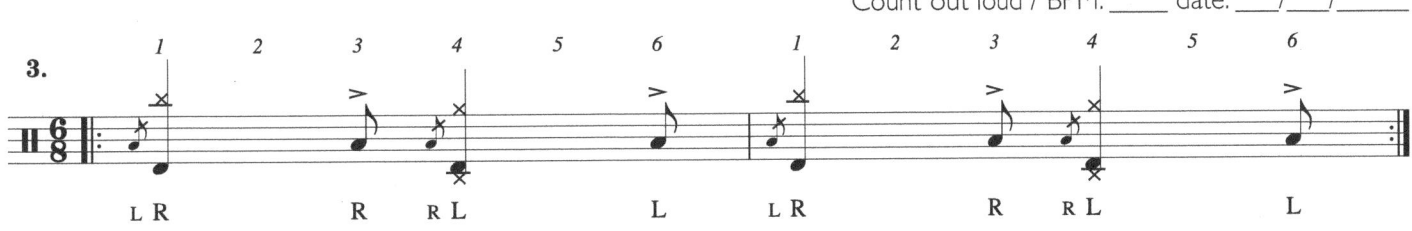

LESSON 104
The Flam Accent

Rhythmic model:

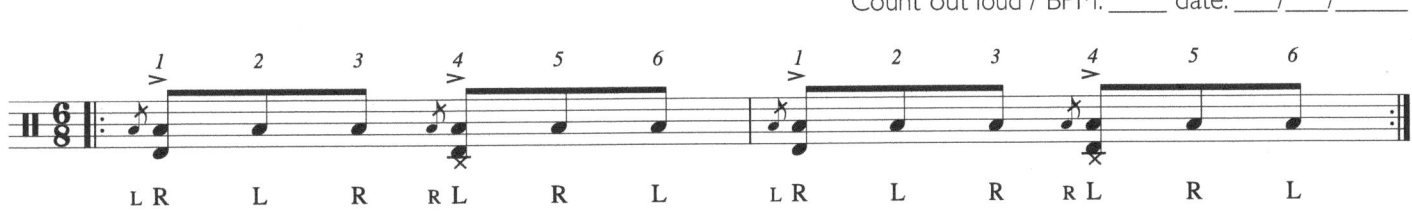

With *1* and *4* on tom-toms:

With *1* and *4* on the floor tom and tom:

Combine 1 & 2:

3.

With initial accents on crash cymbals:

4.

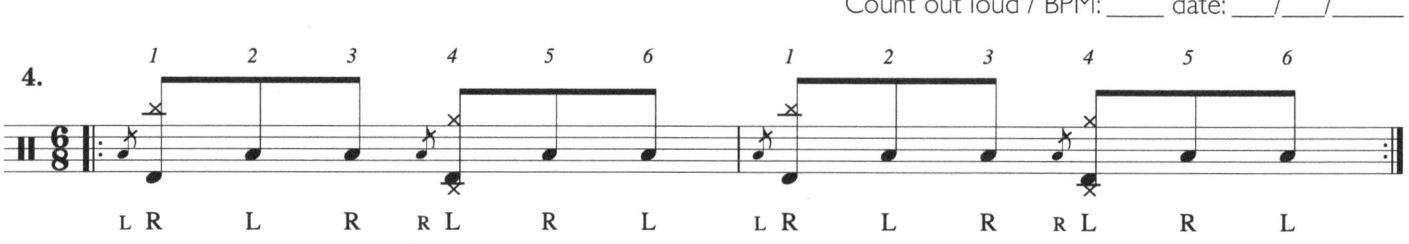

LESSON 105
The Flamacue

Rhythmic model:

Place second accented stroke on tom-toms:

1.

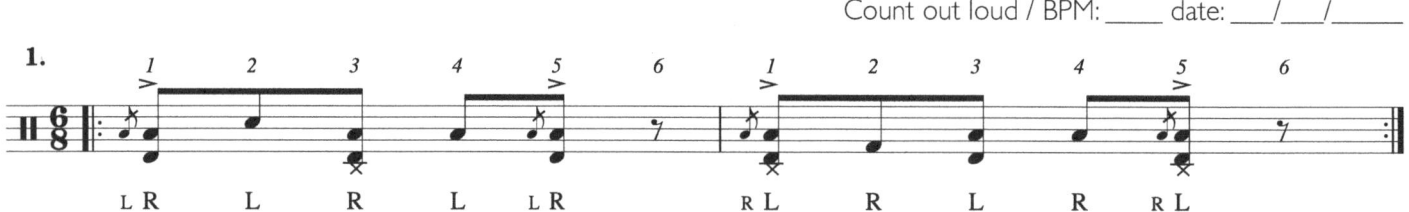

Reverse, with second accented stroke on the snare drum:

2.

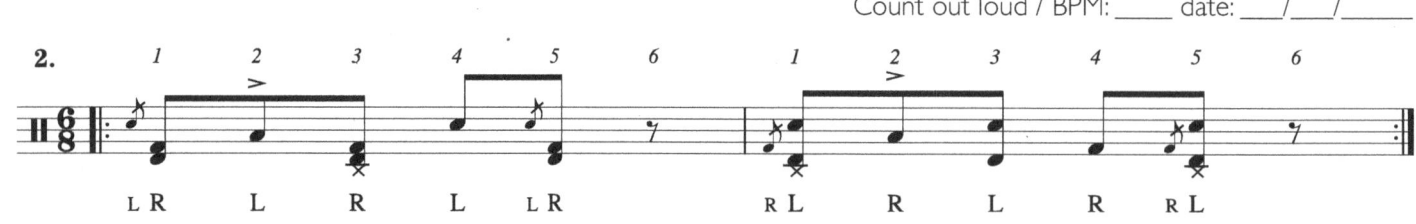

With second accented stroke on crash cymbals:

LESSON 106
The Half Drag (A)

Rhythmic model:

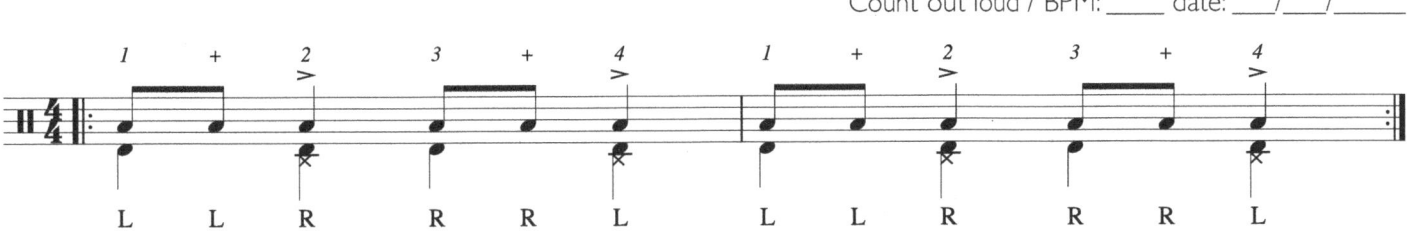

With accented strokes on tom-toms:

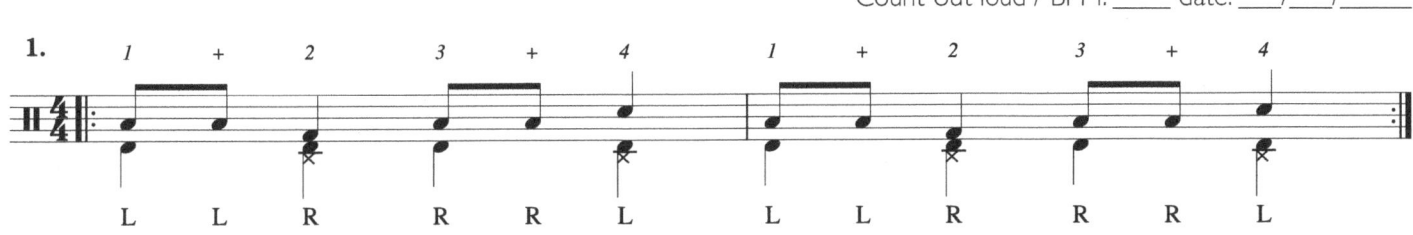

Reverse, with accented strokes on snare drum:

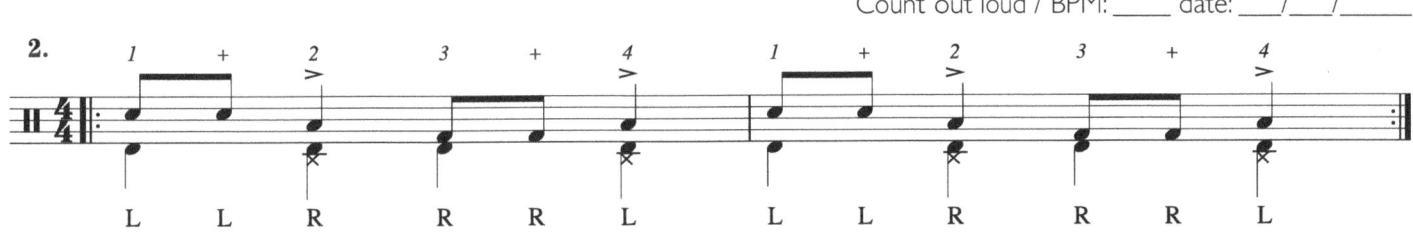

Combine 1 & 2:

With accented strokes on crash cymbals:

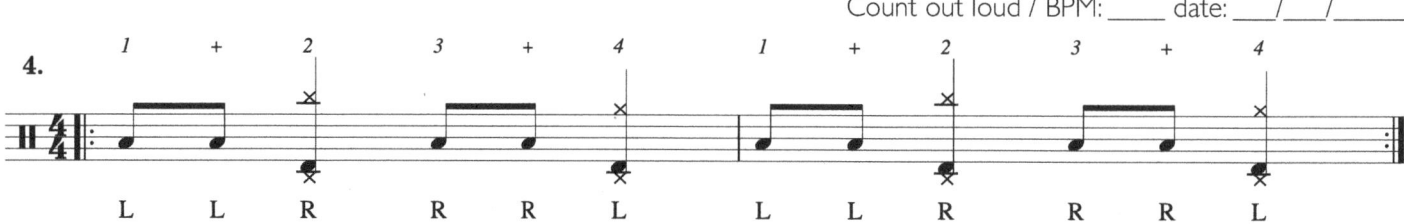

LESSON 107
The Single Drag

Rhythmic model:

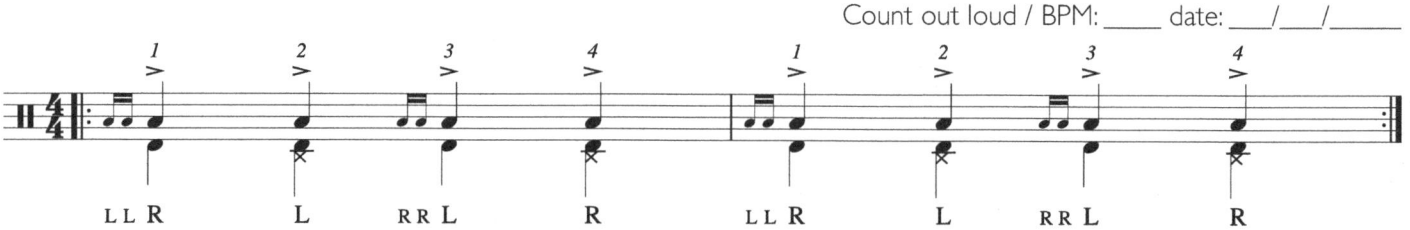

With accented strokes on tom-tom:

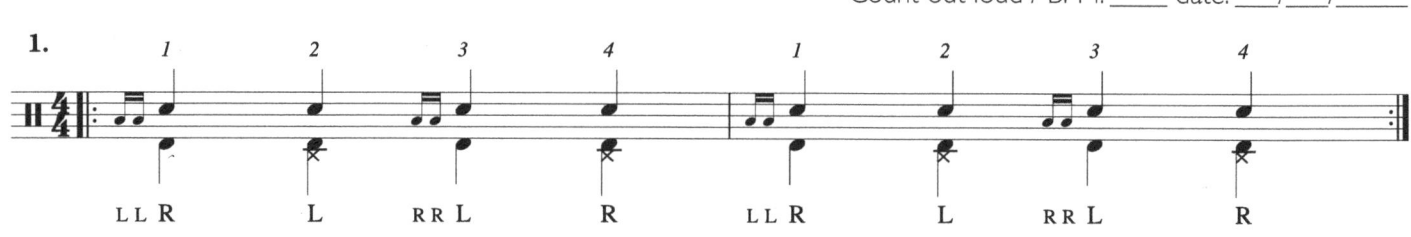

With accents on tom-tom and floor tom:

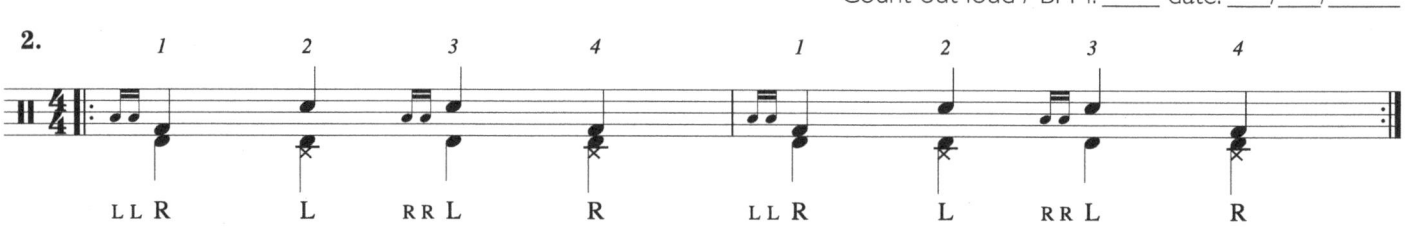

Combine 1 & 2:

With accented beats to crash cymbals:

LESSON 108
The Full Drag

Rhythmic model:

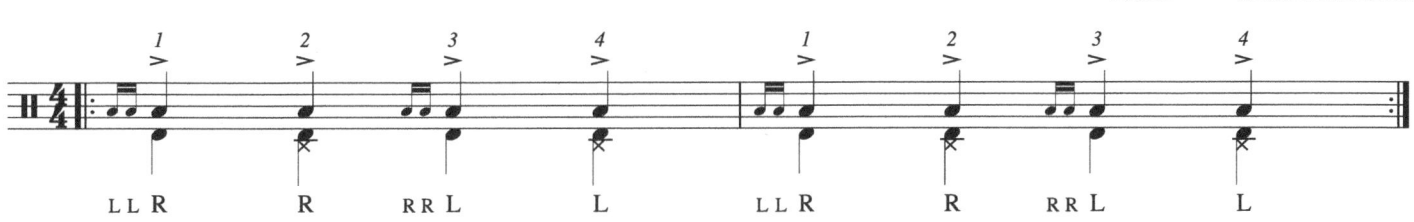

Accented beats to tom:

Accented beats to floor tom and tom:

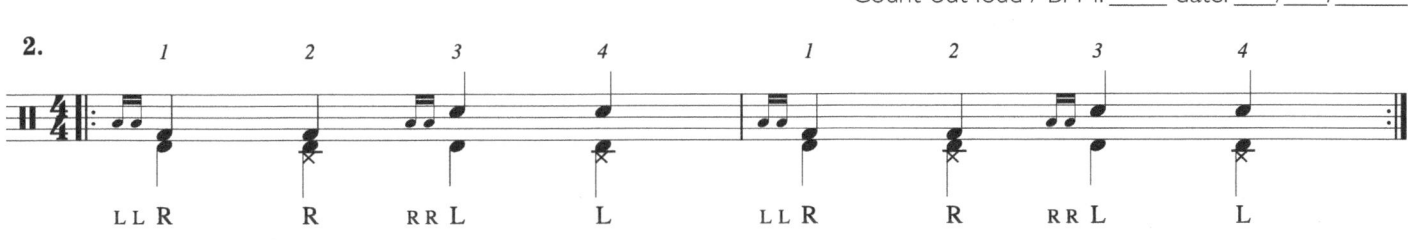

Combine 1 & 2:

LESSON 109
The Double Drag

Rhythmic model:

With *1* and *2* on tom-toms:

With third beat on tom-toms:

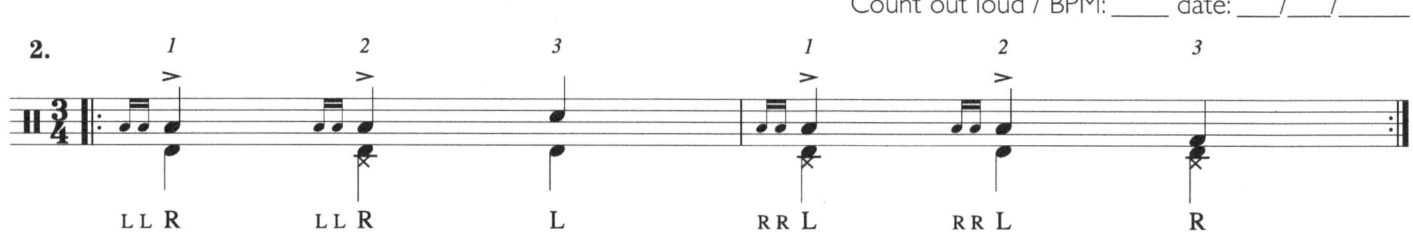

Combine 1 & 2:

LESSON 110
The Single Drag Paradiddle

Rhythmic model:

With initial accent on tom-toms:

LESSON 111
The Double Drag Paradiddle

Rhythmic model:

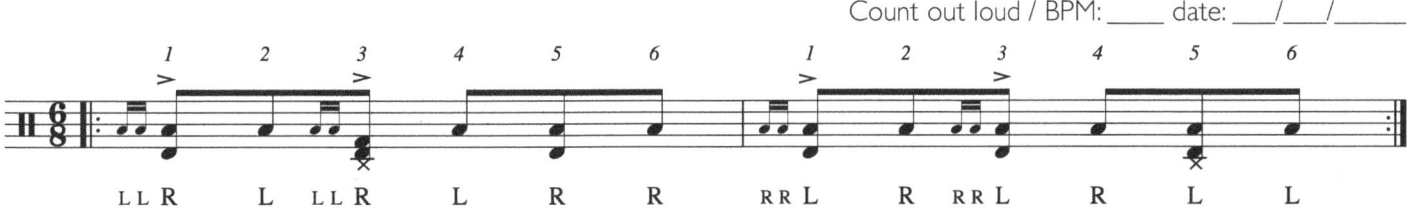

With accents to tom-toms:

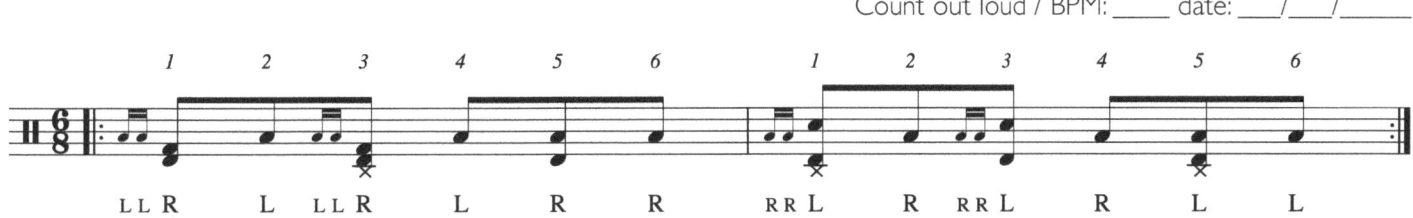

LESSON 112
The Triple Drag Paradiddle

Rhythmic model:

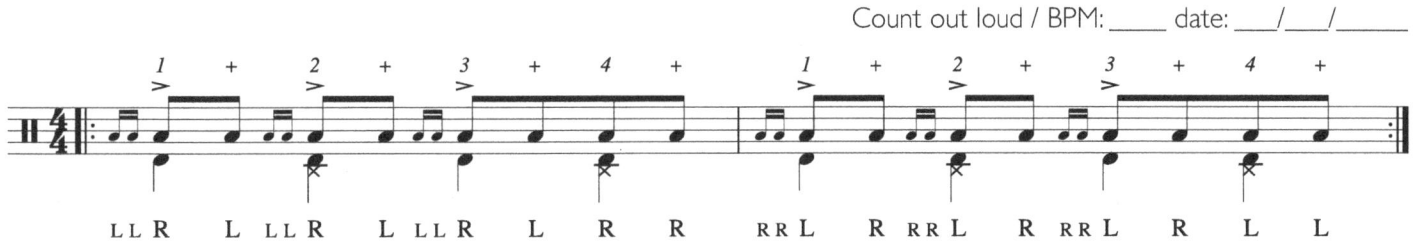

With accents to the tom-toms:

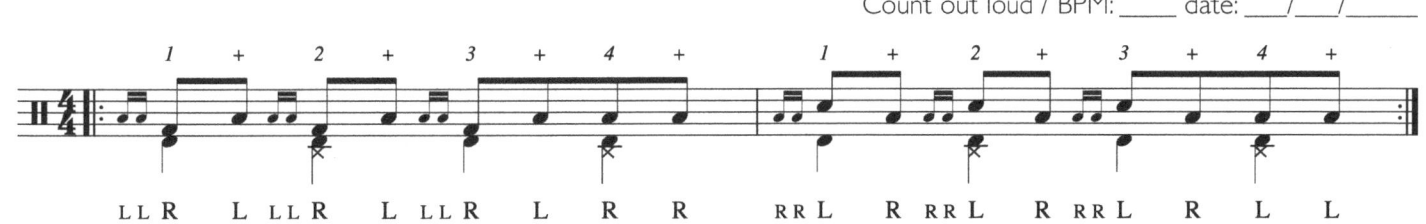

LESSON 113
The Three-Stroke Ruff Single Paradiddle

Rhythmic model:

Share ruff with snare and tom:

1.

Share ruff with tom and floor tom:

2.

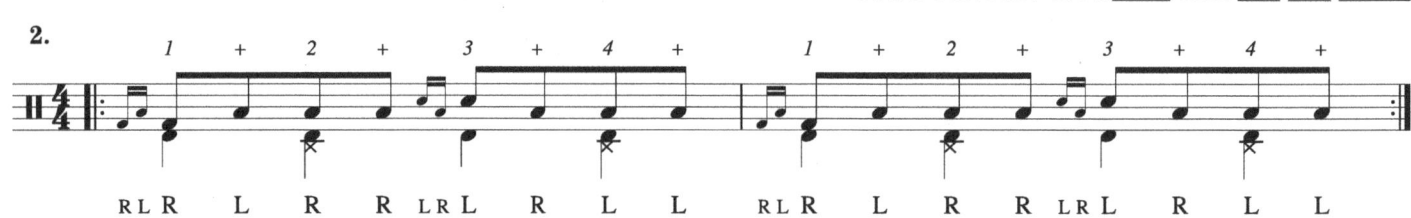

Combine 1 & 2:

3.

LESSON 114
The Three-Stroke Ruff Double Paradiddle (A)

Rhythmic model:

Share ruff with snare and tom:

Share ruff with snare, floor tom and tom:

Combine 1 & 2:

LESSON 115
The Three-Stroke Ruff Double Paradiddle (B)

Rhythmic model:

Share ruff with snare and tom:

107

Share ruff with snare floor tom and tom:

Combine 1 & 2:

LESSON 116
The Three-Stroke Ruff Triple Paradiddle

Rhythmic model:

Share ruff with snare and tom:

Share ruff with snare, floor tom and tom:

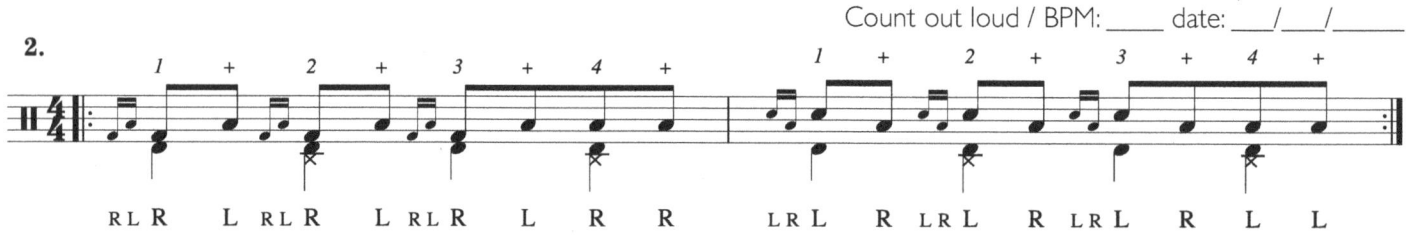

Combine 1 & 2:

3.

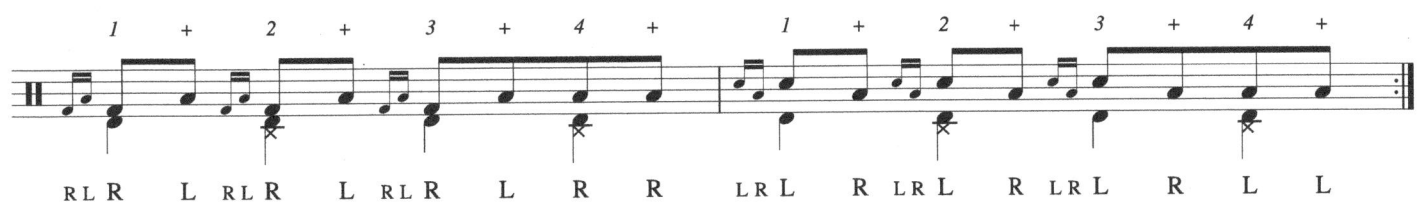

LESSON 117
The Four-Stroke Ruff Single Paradiddle

Rhythmic model:

With four-stroke ruffs sharing snare drum and tom:

1.

Share ruff with floor tom and tom:

2.

Combine 1 & 2:

LESSON 118
The Four-Stroke Ruff Double Paradiddle (A)

Rhythmic model:

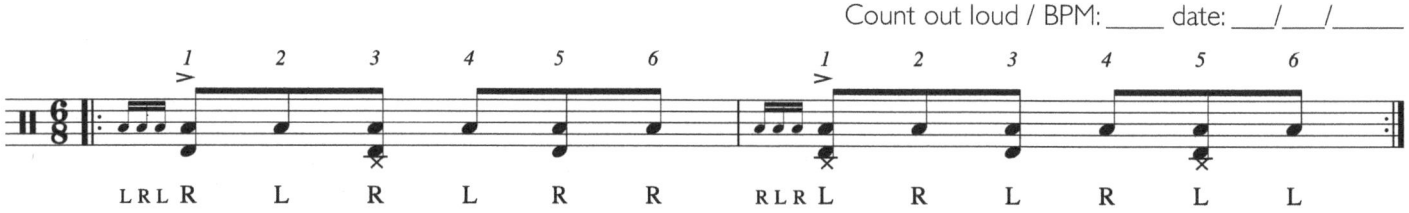

With four-stroke ruffs sharing snare drum and tom:

Share ruff with floor tom and tom:

Combine 1 & 2:

LESSON 119
The Four-Stroke Ruff Double Paradiddle (B)

Rhythmic model:

With four-stroke ruffs sharing snare drum and tom:

1.

Share ruff with snare, floor tom and tom:

2.

Combine 1 & 2:

3.

LESSON 120
The Four-Stroke Ruff Triple Paradiddle

Rhythmic model:

With four-stroke ruffs sharing snare drum and tom:

Share ruff with snare, floor tom and tom:

Combine 1 & 2:

LESSON 121
The Single Ratamacue (A)

This rudiment is a triplet.

Rhythmic model:

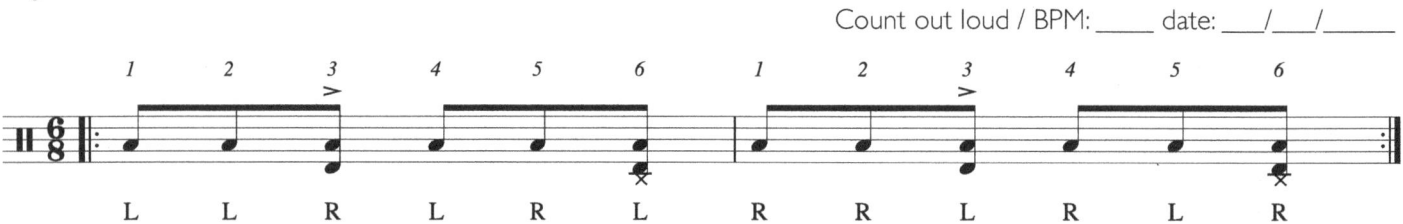

With third stroke on tom:

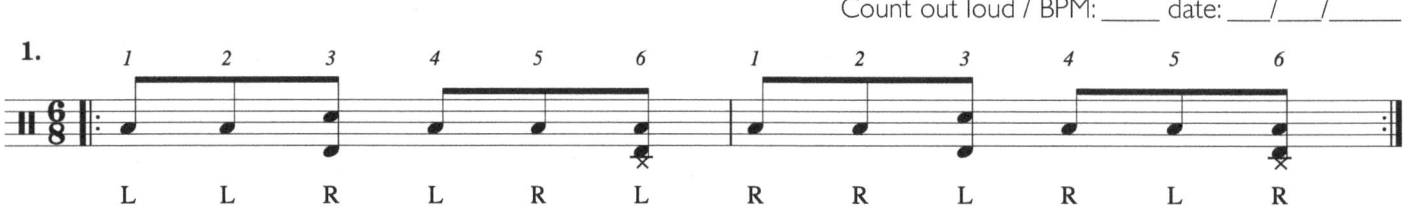

112

With third stroke on floor tom and tom:

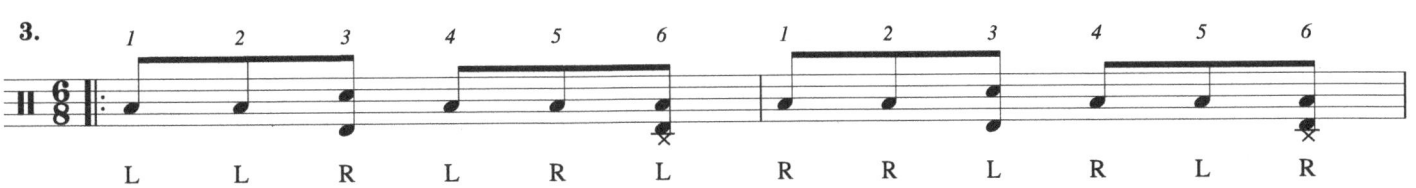

Combine 1 & 2:

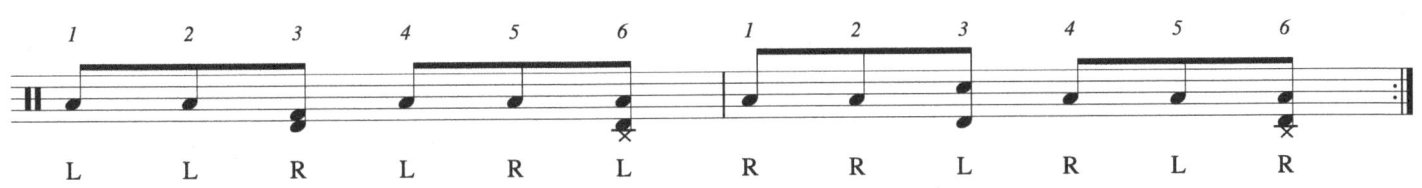

LESSON 122
The Single Ratamacue (B)

Rhythmic model:

With sixth stroke on tom:

With sixth stroke on tom and floor tom:

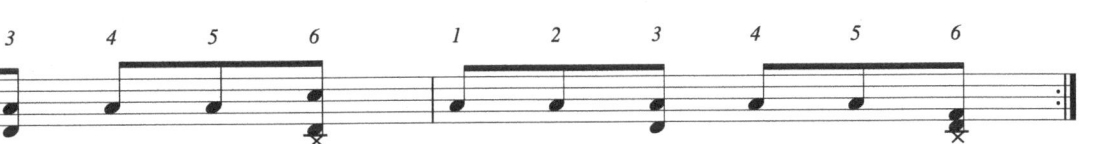

Combine 1 & 2:

Count out loud / BPM: _____ date: ___/___/_____

3.
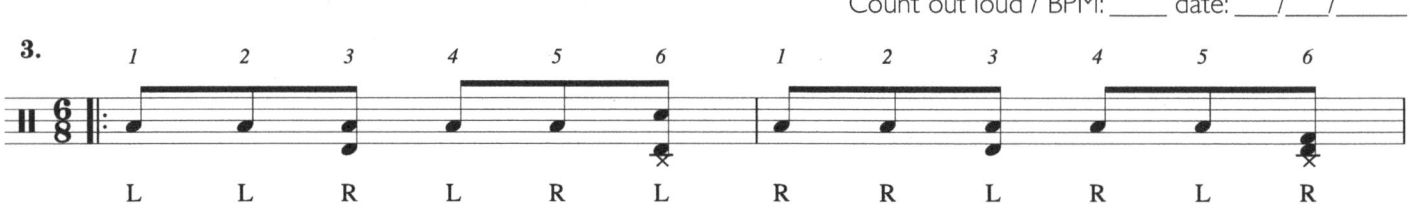

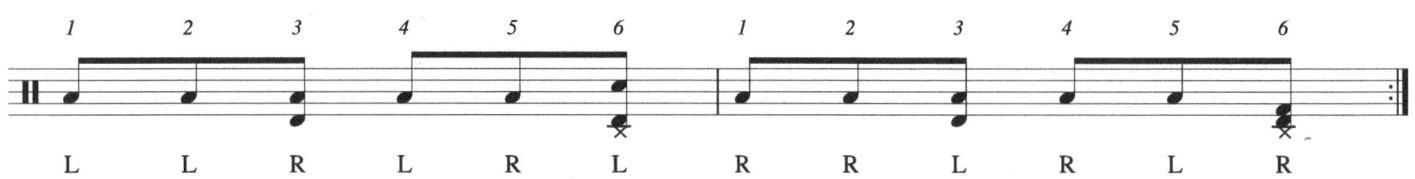

LESSON 123
Combine the Single Ratamacue (A) and (B)

Count out loud / BPM: _____ date: ___/___/_____

1.
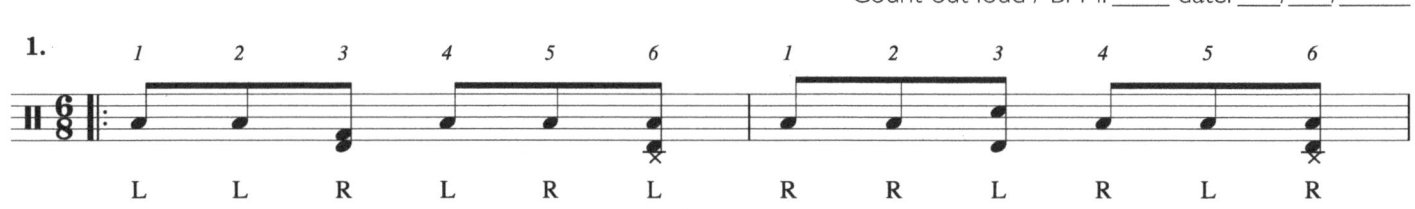

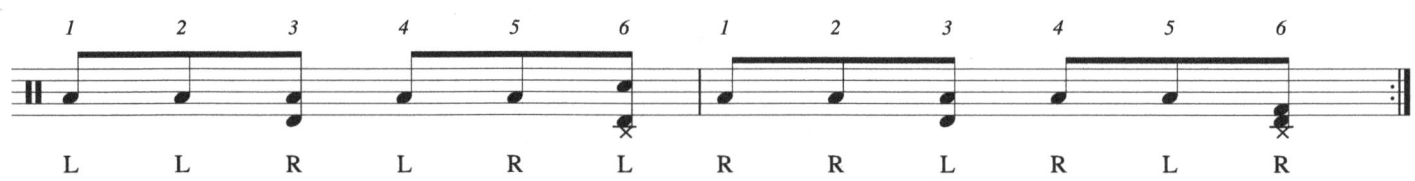

Reverse, with snare receiving accent on third and sixth strokes:

Count out loud / BPM: _____ date: ___/___/_____

2.

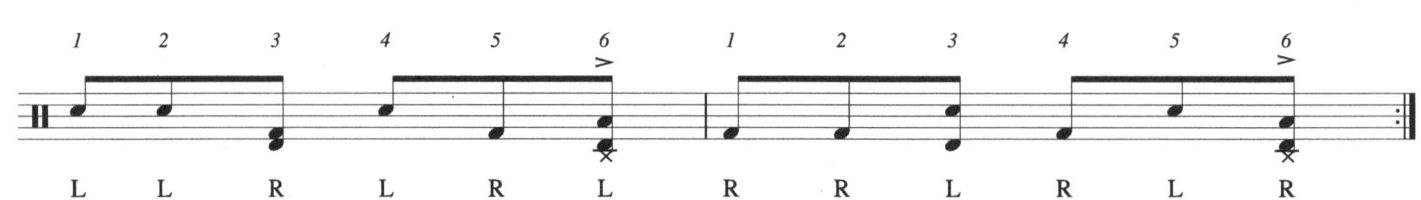

114

LESSON 124

The Single Ratamacue Around the Kit

Clockwise around the kit:

Counterclockwise around the kit:

Combine 1 & 2:

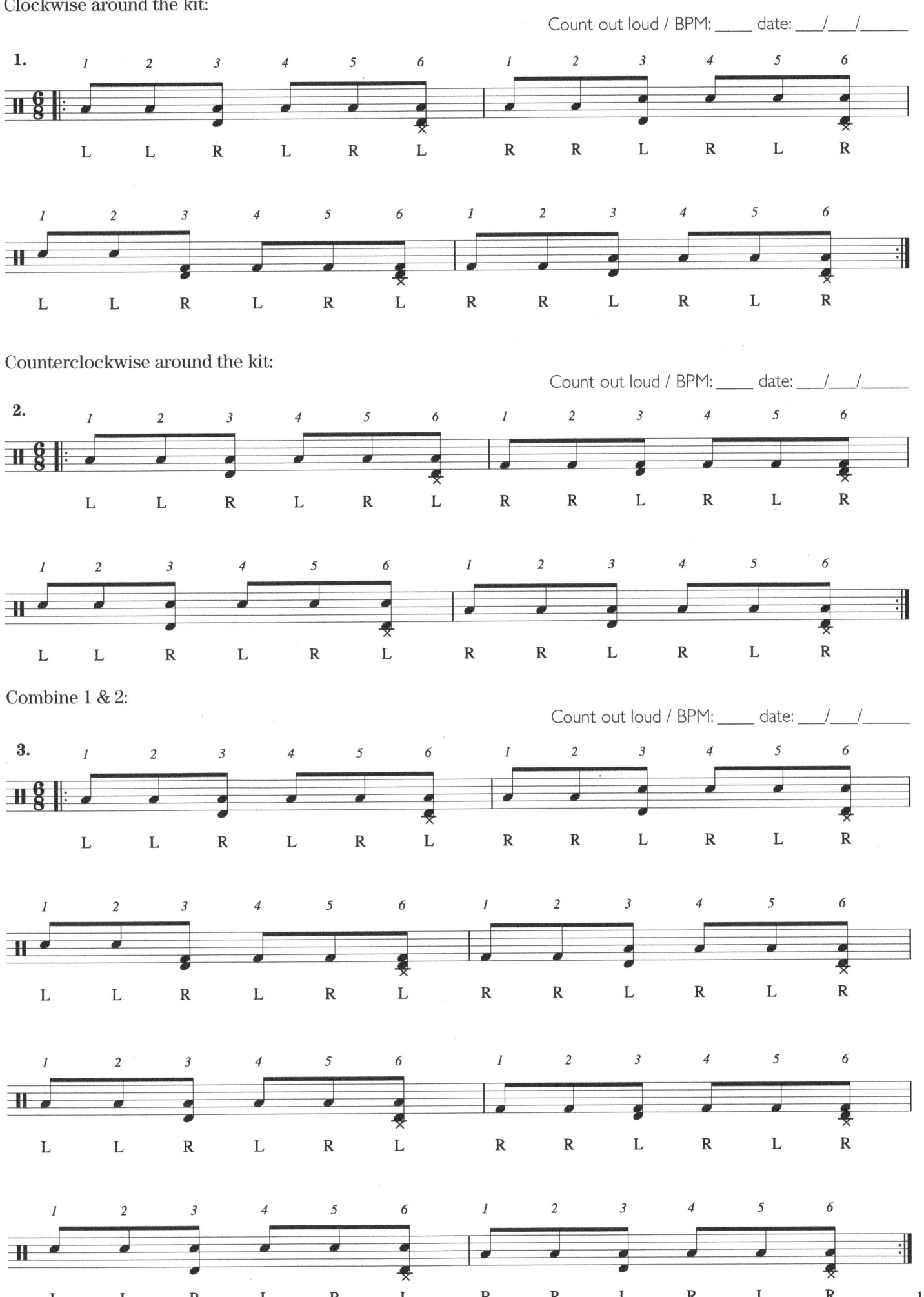

115

LESSON 125
The Single Ratamacue

With "diddles" on snare:

Count out loud / BPM: _____ date: ___/___/_____

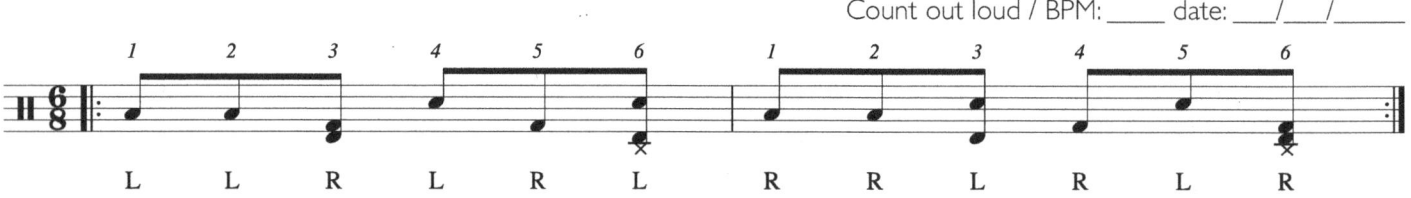

LESSON 126
The Single Ratamacue

With "diddles" on toms:

Count out loud / BPM: _____ date: ___/___/_____

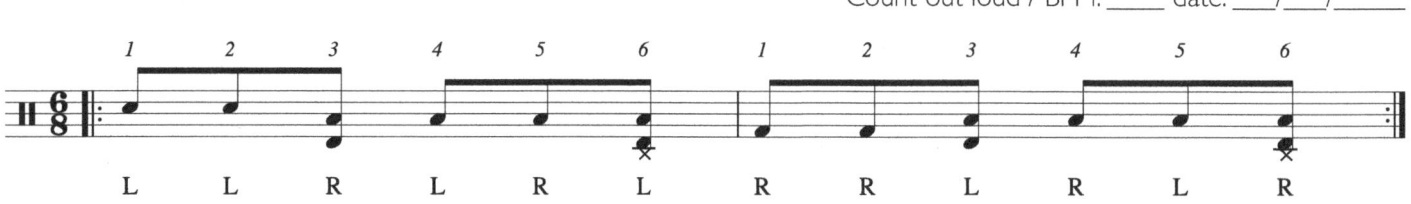

LESSON 127
The Single Ratamacue

Snare and bass drum:

Count out loud / BPM: _____ date: ___/___/_____

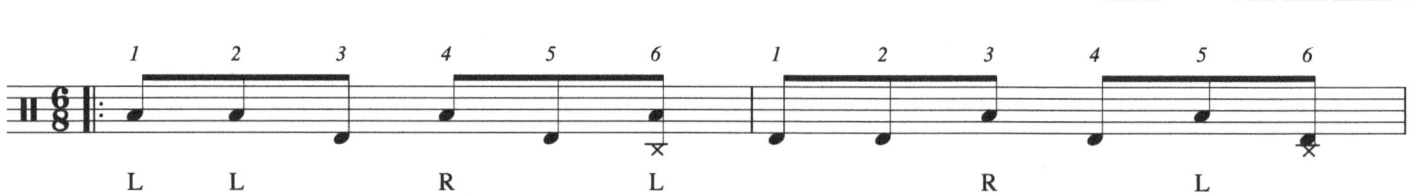

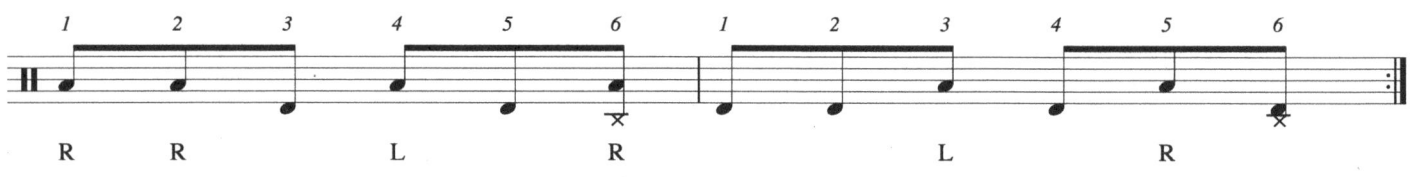

LESSON 128
Combine the Single Ratamacue (A) and (B)

With cymbal crashes on accents. Feather the bass drum, accenting on cymbal crashes.

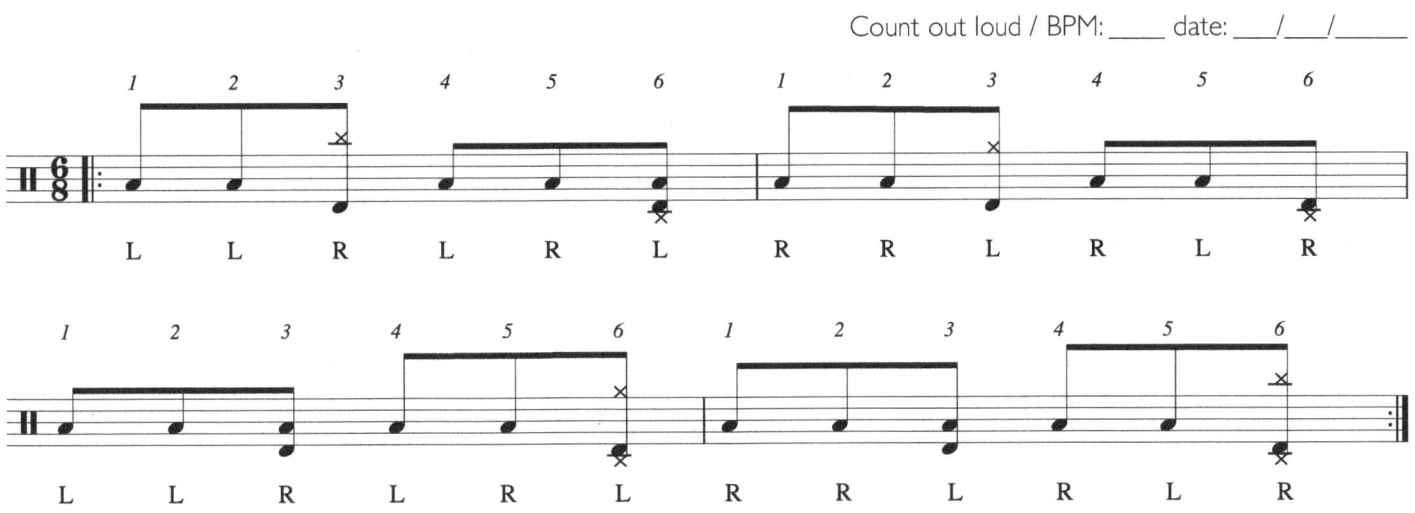

LESSON 129
The Double Ratamacue (A)

Rhythmic model:

With third and sixth strokes on tom-toms:

LESSON 130
The Double Ratamacue (B)

Rhythmic model:

With third and ninth strokes on tom-toms:

LESSON 131
Combine the Double Ratamacue (A) and (B)

Rhythmic model:

With accented strokes to the tom-toms:

Reverse, with accented strokes on snare drum:

LESSON 132
Combine the Double Ratamacue (A) and (B)

With cymbal crashes on accents:

LESSON 133
The Double Ratamacue

Snare and bass drum:

LESSON 134
The Triple Ratamacue (A)

Rhythmic model:

With accented strokes on tom-toms:

1.

LESSON 135
The Triple Ratamacue (B)

Rhythmic model:

With accented strokes on the tom-toms:

1.

LESSON 136
Combine the Triple Ratamacue (A) and (B)

Reverse to toms with accented strokes on snare drum:

LESSON 137
The Triple Ratamacue (A) and (B)

With crashes on the accents:

Count out loud / BPM: ____ date: ___/___/____

LESSON 138
The Triple Ratamacue

Snare and bass drum:

Count out loud / BPM: ____ date: ___/___/____

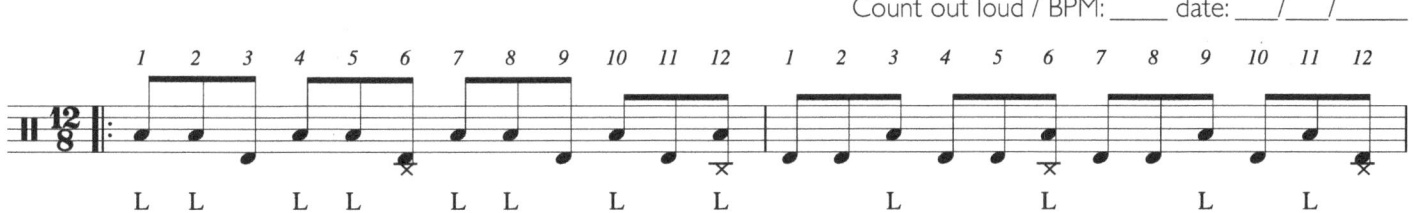

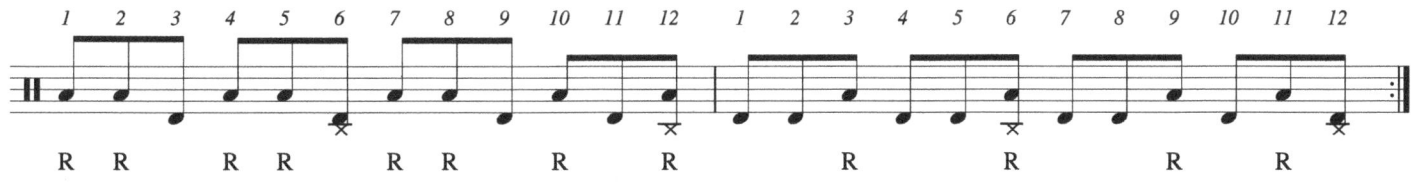

LESSON 139
The Compound Stroke (A)

Accenting the half drag.

Rhythmic model:

With accent on tom-toms:

LESSON 140
The Compound Stroke (B)

Accenting the three-stroke ruff.

Rhythmic model:

With accents on tom-toms:

LESSON 141
Combination of the Two Previous Compound Strokes

Rhythmic model:

Count out loud / BPM: _____ date: ___/___/_____

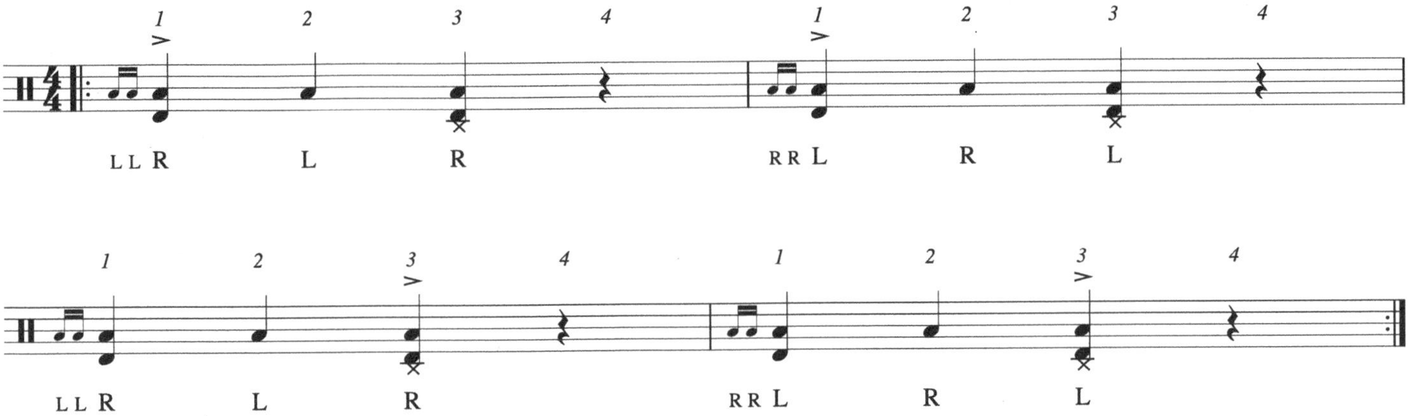

With accents on tom-toms:

Count out loud / BPM: _____ date: ___/___/_____

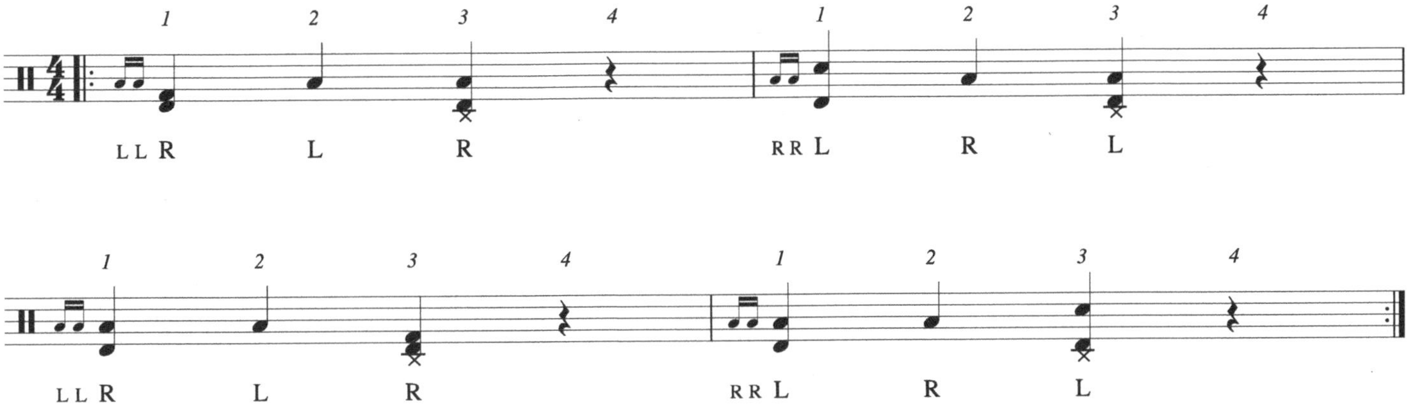

LESSON 142
The Compound Stroke (C)

Rhythmic model:

Count out loud / BPM: _____ date: ___/___/_____

With accents on tom toms:

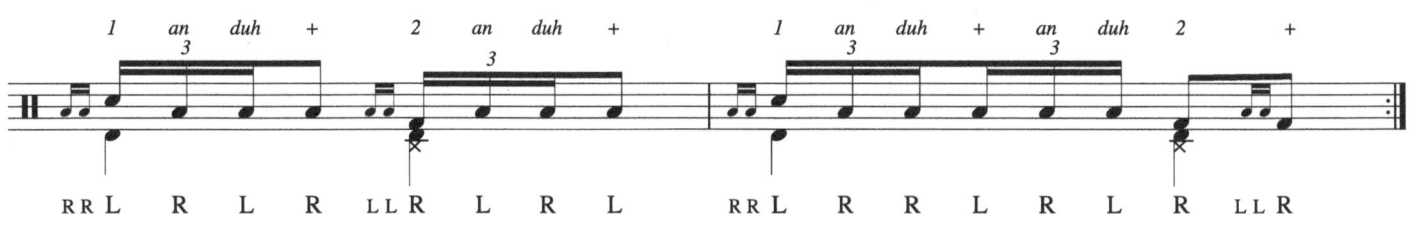

LESSON 143
The Compound Stroke (D)

Rhythmic model:

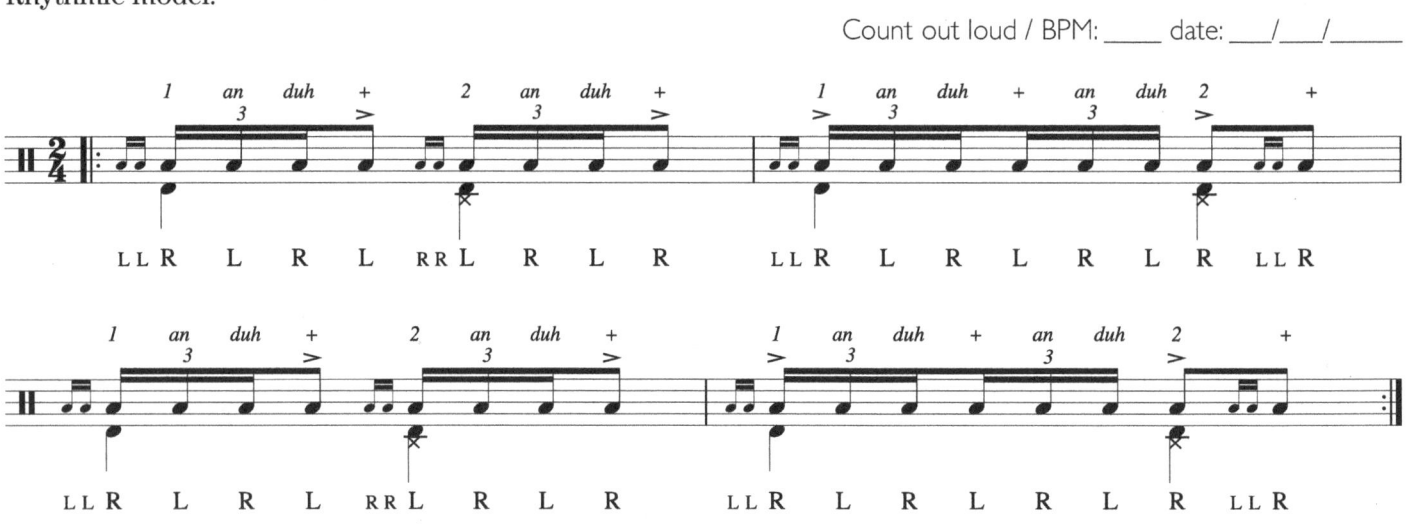

With accents on tom-toms:

LESSON 144
Exercises in Triplets

A *triplet* is a group of three equal notes played in the time ordinarily occupied by two notes of the same value.

A simple way to remember the evenness with which a triplet is to be played is to pronounce the word "e-ven-ly" during its rendition.

Exercise 1

Count out loud / BPM: _____ date: ___/___/_____

Exercise 2

Count out loud / BPM: _____ date: ___/___/_____

Exercise 3

Count out loud / BPM: _____ date: ___/___/_____

Exercise 4

Exercise 5

Exercise 6

Exercise 7

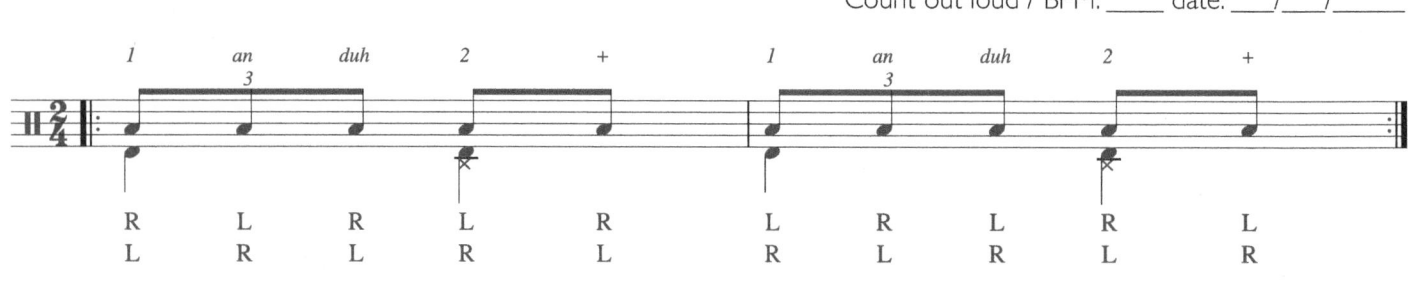

Exercise 8 (Drag triplets)

Count out loud / BPM: _____ date: ___/___/_____

Exercise 9 (Drag triplets)

Count out loud / BPM: _____ date: ___/___/_____

Exercise 10 (Drag triplets)

Count out loud / BPM: _____ date: ___/___/_____

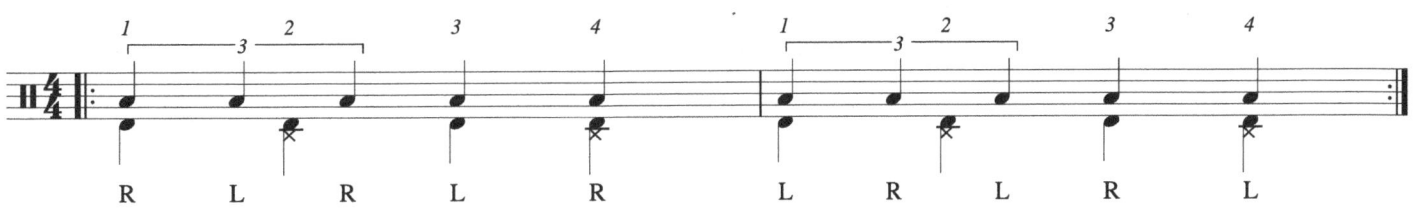

DEDICATION

While at Berklee College of Music in the late sixties, a fellow drummer let me in on his studies with Henry Adler. I suddenly realized my shortcomings and eventually secured Henry as my drum teacher. For starters, my hands were not turning properly. As Henry would say, "You're working too hard!"

As I began studying with Henry, I became immersed in his teaching. Every lesson was inspiring as he pressed me to his higher standard. He shared amazing stories and was very generous with his time. After a year of studying with "The Master," my skills were transformed to a level previously unattainable.

Henry Adler was an accomplished drummer, studio musician, author, publisher, manufacturer, entrepreneur, teacher. Some of the greats Henry taught where Dave Tough; Sonny Igoe; Roy Burns; Alvin Stoller; Louie Bellson; Sandy Feldstein; and "The World's Greatest Drummer," Buddy Rich.

In 1942, Buddy Rich collaborated with Henry Adler in writing *Buddy Rich's Modern Interpretation of Snare Drum Rudiments*. *Buddy Rich's Rudiments Around the Kit* applies these rudiments from the original book to the drum set. I would like to dedicate this work in memory of Henry Adler.

—Ted MacKenzie